19 PLUS TIPS FOR USING GMAIL TO THE FULLEST: GMAIL AUTOMATION AND USING THIRD PARTY TOOLS

K.Koushik

Published by Koushik K, 2016.

While every precaution has been taken in the preparation of this book, the publisher assumes no responsibility for errors or omissions, or for damages resulting from the use of the information contained herein.

19 PLUS TIPS FOR USING GMAIL TO THE FULLEST: GMAIL AUTOMATION AND USING THIRD PARTY TOOLS

First edition. April 27, 2016.

Copyright © 2016 K.Koushik.

ISBN: 979-8201500467

Written by K.Koushik.

Table of Contents

Introduction

Hello, thank you for purchasing this eBook. Through this book, you are going to learn some nice features of Gmail in detail which you may have not noticed even if you use Gmail as your email provider.

I assume that you already have an email account in Gmail. You can sign up easily even if you don't have so I am not covering the basic stuff like composing emails, using the Gmail's text editor etc. If you need help with that stuff, feel free to contact me.

You may have noticed the features but you may need some guidance for using those features with ease or to learn multiple ways to access a feature etc then this book will definitely be of help to you.

This book also covers the use of some third party plug-ins and add-ons to make Gmail more efficient. Using filters for automation and semi automation of tasks, using the advance search function of Gmail etc will help you speed up and also work with ease.

If you feel you want me to explain a feature for you. Or if you get a doubt, you can feel free to contact me through my email. (Given in contact me page)

Performing bulk actions on Gmail

Sometimes you may want to move emails to spam, delete or archive many emails at bulk you can do it by using the checkboxes

Below is the view of your Gmail inbox

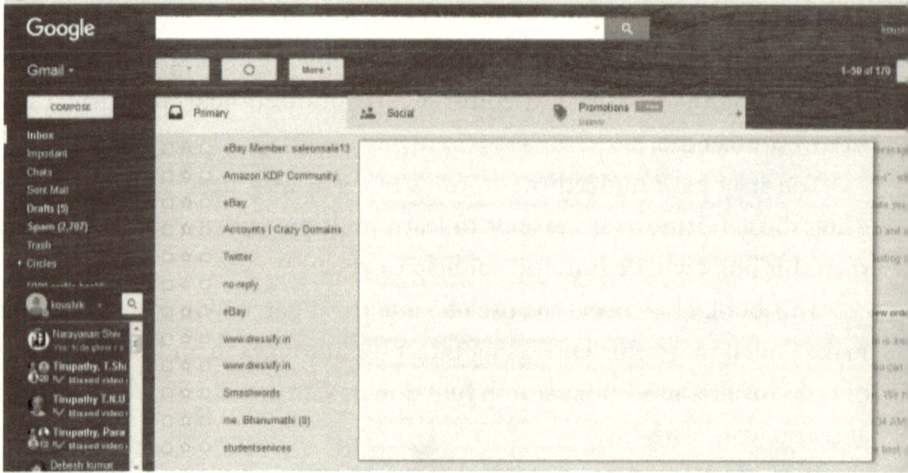

As soon as you tick the check box you will see a bar appear above your messages folder or section (we take inbox for this example) as shown below

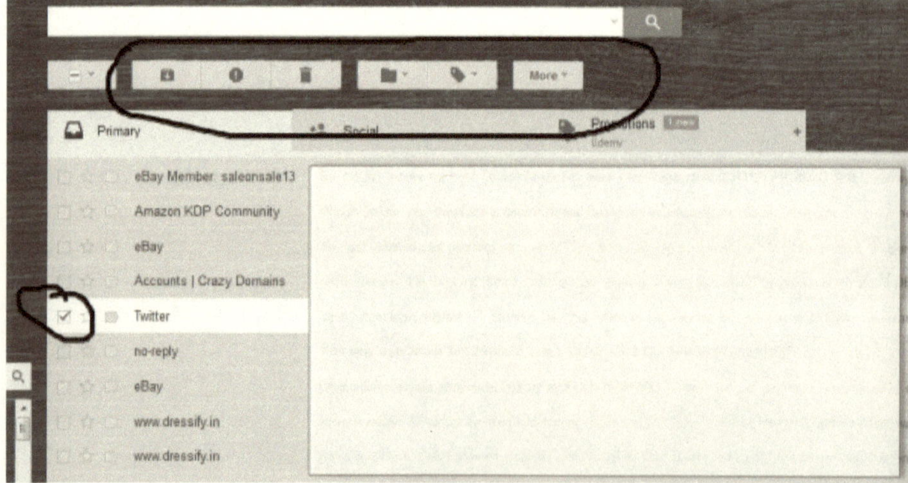

19 PLUS TIPS FOR USING GMAIL TO THE FULLEST: GMAIL AUTOMATION AND USING THIRD PARTY TOOLS

To select multiple emails you can click the checkbox one by one

To select a continuous series of email to perform some action, select the first check box in the series. Now holding the shift key, select the last continuous email and release the shift key. If you want to continue the selection after leaving the next two subsequent emails and then select a continuous series of email you can do it following the same process.

Primary		Social
Amazon KDP Community		Watch update:
Amazon KDP Community		Watch update:
eBay Member: saleonsale13		Re: I didn't recei
Amazon KDP Community		Watch update: r
eBay		You just updatec
Accounts | Crazy Domains		rawdietrecipes.ii
Twitter		Your Twitter logii
no-reply		Your new login c
eBay		Confirmation of y
www.dressify.in		[www.dressify.in

Let me explain you with an example

Say there are ten emails in the inbox and you want to select the first five emails click the checkbox on the left of the first email. Hold the shift key and click the checkbox left to the fifth email

Now if you want to leave the email six and seven and select the rest of the emails, select the eighth email by clicking the checkbox, then select the tenth email while holding shift key.

To select all the emails in that page, click the check box which is above the mailbox

All the email you see in that page will be selected. Once you move or delete the selected email (we will learn this later in this chapter) you will see the other emails present in the folder.

Sometimes you may wish to select all the emails of the folder so that you can empty the folder or do some other action. For that you should click the checkbox above the folder and then click the link select all 200 conversations in primary (for example) or a similar link at the top as shown in the below image.

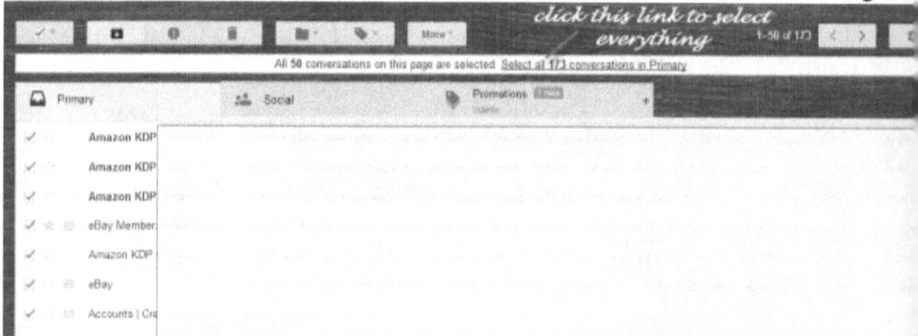

Then you can perform the desired action by clicking the icons as shown before.

There are also more options available for selection you can access them by clicking the small down arrow button near the checkbox at top

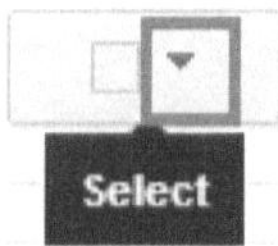

The options you will see are shown below

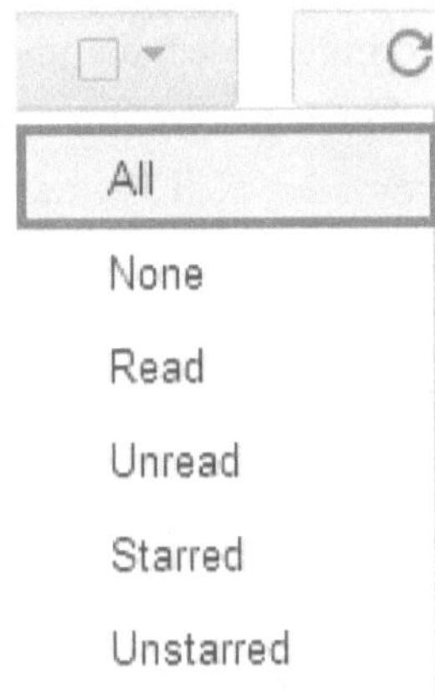

All selects all the messages in the page

None deselects all the messages in the page

Read selects all the messages you have already opened

Unread selects all the messages which have not been opened and viewed by you

Starred selects all that emails which has been starred as important

Unstarred selects all the messages which are not starred

Now you may want to know what a starred message is

You can star an email by clicking the star symbol on the left side of an email.

Or by clicking the star symbol in the right side of the email message near the date (while the message is open) this helps you categorize the emails which you think is important, we will discuss more about categorizing in a later chapter.

Now let us see the buttons which appear after you select the emails.

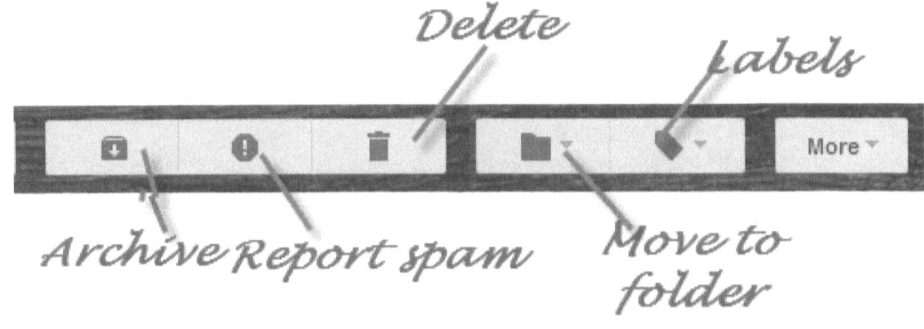

Archive: when you press this button after selecting the emails all the selected emails will be put in to archive, (i.e.) they will be moved from your inbox and put into all mails section. If you find an email which is not very important but you think you may need it for reference in late future you can put them in the archive. The mail will not be deleted but it will disappear from the inbox. This is helpful in clearing your inbox but in my opinion folders are a better option. (We will discuss about folders in a separate chapter)

How to access an archived mail?

You can access an archived mail in the all mail section in from the navigation slide bar in the left side, below your labels and above the starred link.

You can also access all mail section by typing all mail in the search bar and pressing enter key.

Report spam/ mark as spam: by clicking this button, selected email will be moved to spam. All the future emails sent from that email address will also automatically be moved to spam. So please use this button wisely only when it is actually needed.

Please check the spam folder every 15-20 days and do a quick scroll to see if you find anything important there. If you find an email which is not spam, you can select that particular email from the spam folder and mark it as not spam. The email goes back to inbox.

I asked you to check the spam folder once in a while within 15-20 days because if an email stays in spam folder for 30 days it will automatically deleted permanently.

Delete/send to thrash: this button is used to delete emails which you don't need any more the email stays there for 30 days from the date of deletion and then it is permanently deleted.

To get back an email you have accidentally deleted you can go to thrash folder and select the particular email and press move to folder and select inbox

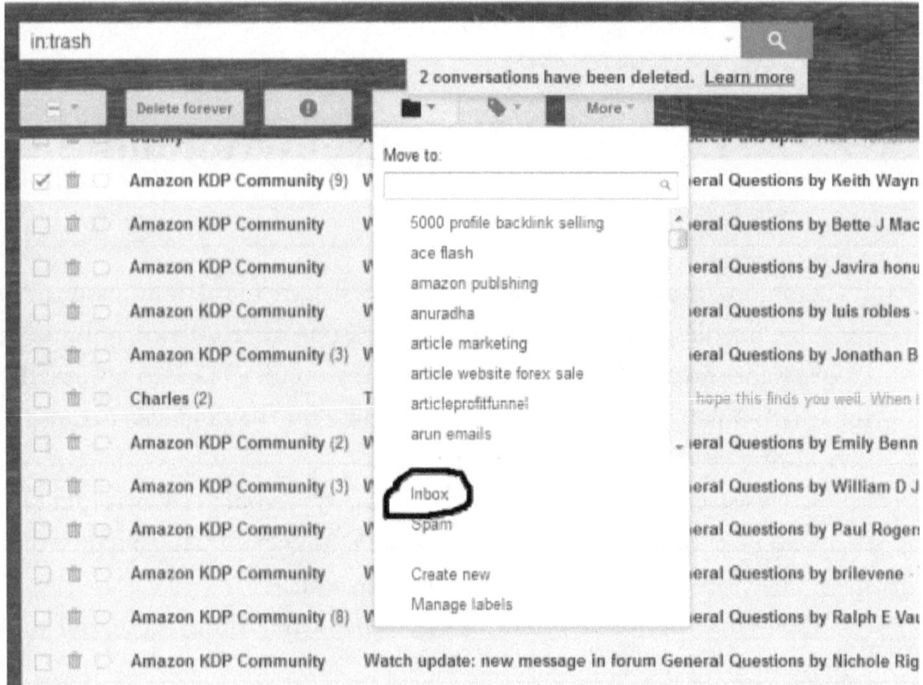

All though we have discussed bulk actions with the help of inbox these are available in all the folders and sections of Gmail.

Dealing with your subscriptions

It's common for us to subscribe to many newsletters for various reasons, maybe for some freebies, free download or other reasons. after a period of time, we no longer want those emails coming to us but it's a tedious task to unsubscribe all the emails one by one since we don't find time for that and also because it is a very boring task.

So we leave those subscribed and delete them in bulk even without reading them. Some even report these emails as spam. It is very unfair to report them as spam since we have subscribed for them with will.

Then what can be the solution? Let's use a free third party tool to mass unsubscribe our subscriptions.

Go to www.unroll.me[1]

Get the get started button

Enter your email and click I agree to the terms and privacy policy and click continue.

Be aware that you will have to share the right to view and manage your email.

View your basic profile info and manage your contacts. I have been using this app for a while and I had no problems.

To be able to use this app you should click allow,

A message says, Wait for a few seconds the scan may take up to two minutes, mine ended within a few seconds. It depends upon your email account's used space, bandwidth of the app and many other factors.

Click continue, it found 40 subscriptions in my Gmail account

After clicking the unsubscribe button in the right of the corresponding newsletters,

Click continue, and then you may share about this app through Facebook and then click finish.

1.	http://www.unroll.me

Then you can log-out of unroll.me by clicking your email address on top right corner of the website and then selecting logout.

You can use this wonderful app from time to time to clean your email from unwanted newsletters.

Using Labels and Categories to organize your email

What is a label and why we should use it.

Labels allow you to organize your email messages into categories. They are similar to folders however, unlike folders; you can apply more than one label to a single message. NOTE: Gmail supports a maximum of 5,000 labels, including sub-labels.

There are two ways to create a new label.

Select an email which you want to put under a label by clicking the check box and then click the labels Icon and click "create new" to create a new label.

Note: you can also put the email in to any label you have already created by choosing the label name.

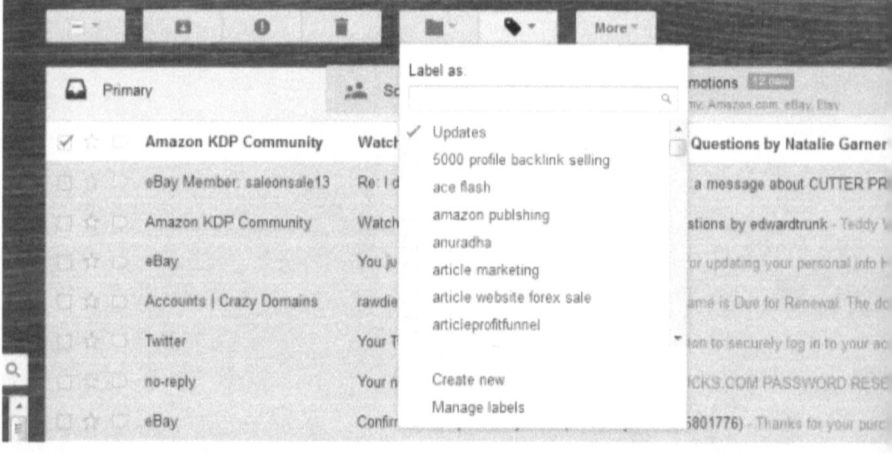

After you click create new, a New Label dialog box will appear

Type in a name you want to create a label with and click create

To label an email or a set of emails with the label you created select the emails and then click the labels icon and select the name of the label from the list of labels and click apply, the emails will be labelled.

Note that even if the emails are labelled it will still stay in your inbox

To move it out of the inbox we will be using the move to folder icon. But before teaching that to you let me show you another way to create label

Another method to create a label

Scroll down and you will find create new label link at the bottom of the navigation slide-bar you can also use that. To create a label

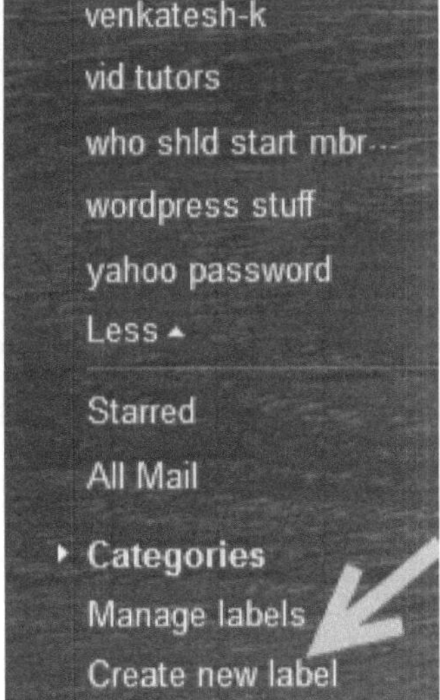

Then use the method which we discussed to put your emails under that label.

Different options in a label

Let us see some of the nice things you can do after labeling your emails

You can give a label color

Go to your navigation slide bar and move your mouse pointer over the label name and then click the small triangle which appears near the label to see more options

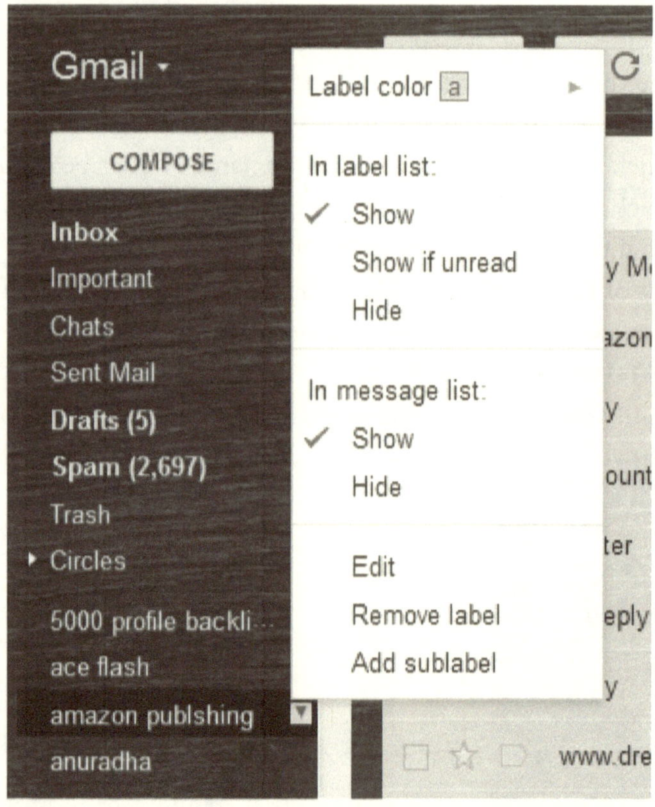

Then you can do a lot of things like giving a label color

See, I have given a red color for my amazon publishing label; this is very helpful for you to see and find the labels in your inbox easily. The inbox will also look colorful.

You can hide a label in message list, so all the emails in that label are hidden from your inbox.

You can find that label from the navigation slide bar and hover your mouse over it, click the little triangle and then click the show option again to make it appear in the inbox

You can also hide a label from labels list.

If Show if unread option is selected, the label appears in the label list only if there are unread messages inside that label.

The easiest method to create a label is to use move to folder

As I already said, placing an email inside a label only adds a label to the email and it doesn't move the email from the inbox. I don't like my labeled emails to stay in my inbox, I always keep my inbox free only for new emails which I have to check, once I check the email, I label it and move it out of my inbox. I feel many amongst you are like me, am I right?

For labeling an email and moving it out of inbox (i.e.) the email disappears from the inbox. That moved email is accessible by searching for the label through search bar or by clicking on the label name from the navigation slide bar. This helps me a lot in keeping my inbox clean and free

If you want to create a new label for a set of emails and label them and move them.

Select the emails by clicking the corresponding checkboxes, click the move to folder icon type the label name in the search bar inside the move to folder icon. It will show a create new link if the label name is not already present see the below image

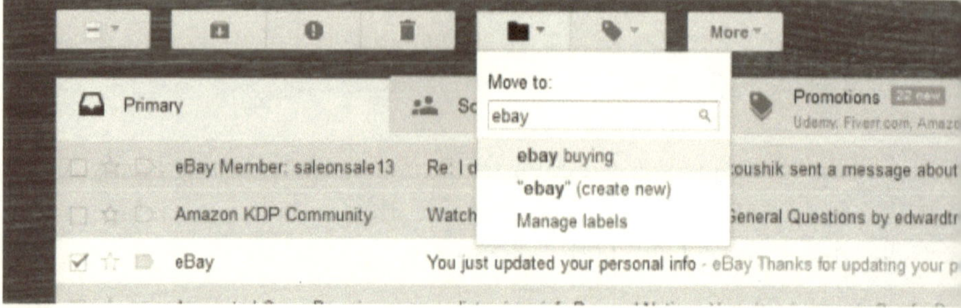

I have selected an email related to eBay, then I select, move to icon and type ebay in the move to -search bar. I already have a label called eBay buying but I don't have a label called ebay so it shows eBay buying and also shows ebay in quotes with a (create new) near it.

I can click that create new link to create the new label named ebay

Click the create new link shown and a create label dialog box appears. Click create

And yes the email you selected has been moved and you will not see it inside your inbox.

Now you select some other email to move to eBay label, click the move to icon and type eBay, this time you will see the label listed there

Which is better? Labels or move to

I prefer move to instead of using labels icon, but there is one single con, there is no use of giving label color if you are going to use move to only.

If you find the features like show, hide etc you will like labels more than move to. If you are used to organizing your emails in folders regularly and you don't like seeing the labeled messages inside inbox, you will be happy with move to feature.

Now that we discussed about labels, let us discuss about categories too.

Categories

Your messages are classified into categories such as Primary, Promotions, Social and Updates. You can choose to use categories as inbox tabs, and as labels. These categories make it easy to focus on messages that are important to you and read messages of the same type all at once.

If you are not already using the categories your Gmail inbox will look like

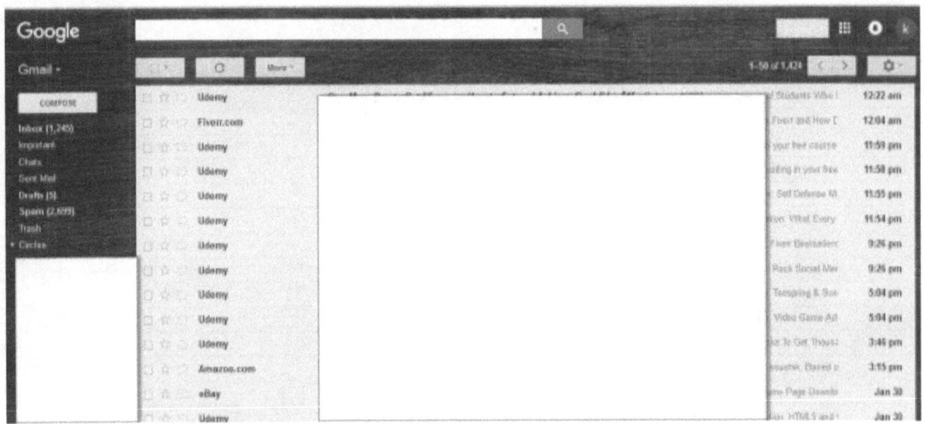

To enable categories, click the gear and select configure inbox

The configure inbox dialog box will appear I have selected primary, social and promotions and also selected include starred messages in primary check box.

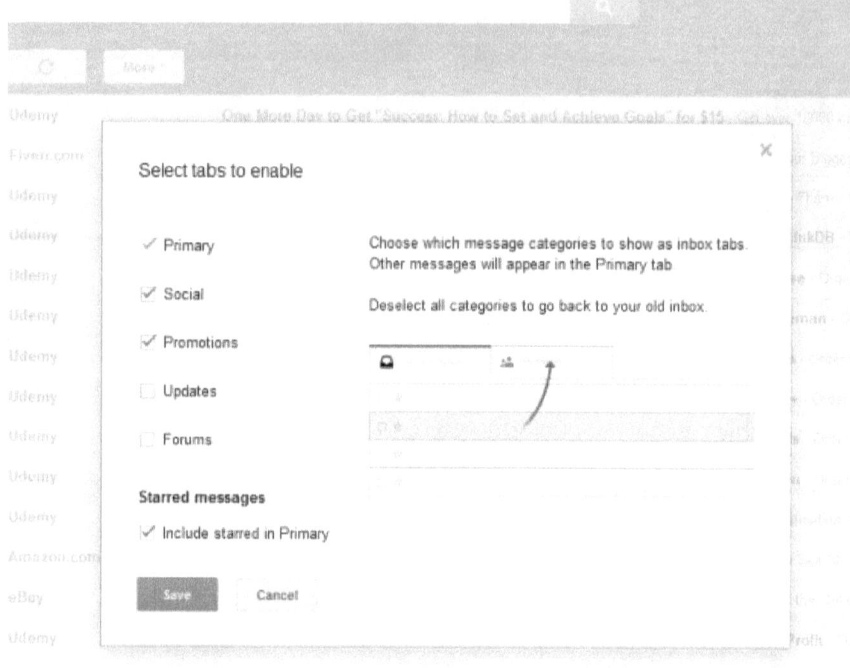

Refer the below image for categories and their use

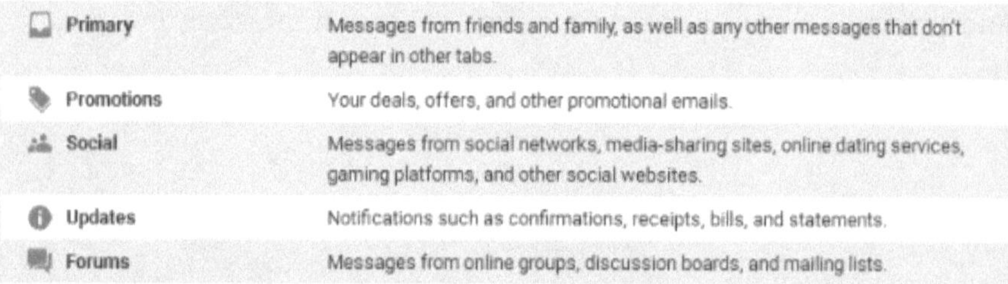

Primary	Messages from friends and family, as well as any other messages that don't appear in other tabs.
Promotions	Your deals, offers, and other promotional emails.
Social	Messages from social networks, media-sharing sites, online dating services, gaming platforms, and other social websites.
Updates	Notifications such as confirmations, receipts, bills, and statements.
Forums	Messages from online groups, discussion boards, and mailing lists.

Select all the categories you feel you need and then click save

We have already discussed about starred emails, starred emails are emails which we feel important and star it so I have selected the option to maintain those in primary

These categories help a great deal in maintaining your inbox clean.

After selecting the categories, you will see these tabs.

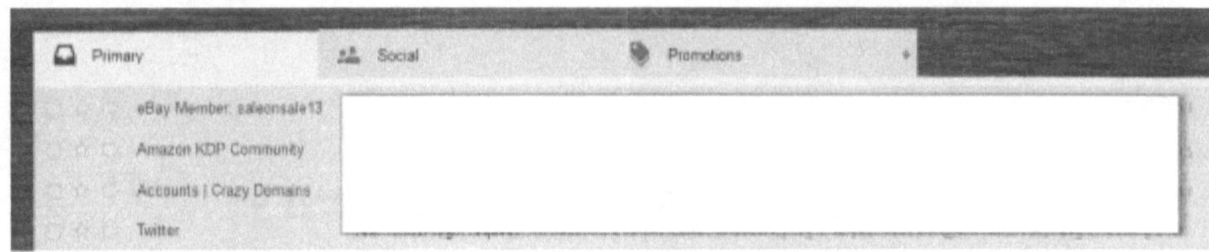

I usually go to promotions very rare, all I do is give a quick glance and bulk delete the emails every once in a while. Also maintaining your social stuff, your Facebook notifications and other things in a separate category is very helpful as you will not be disturbed or distracted by a social network's notification while working. Great feature to me.

Some more about stars

We have already discussed about what stars are in the first chapter of the book while telling you about multiple selection of emails and bulk actions. By now you know what a star is and why we use it.

But we have only discussed about a default yellow star while starring our emails to mark it as an important email.

Do you know? Gmail offers us different stars we will talk about that in this chapter

To enable the use of different stars click the gear button and click settings

Then in general tab (which is the first tab in settings page), scroll down you will find the star settings (shown below)

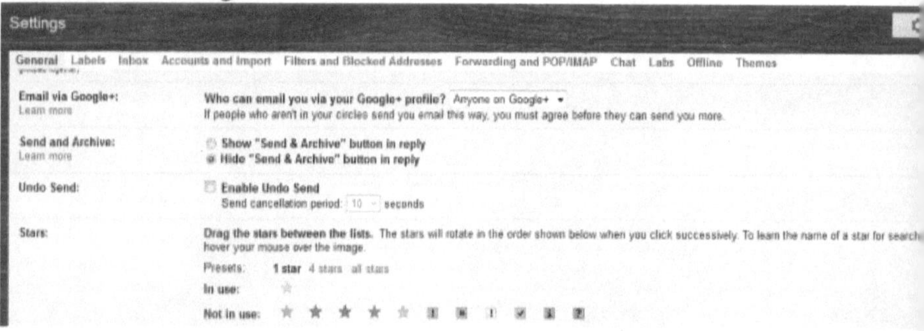

The default is one star

You can click four stars and you will use 4 important stars that are shown below

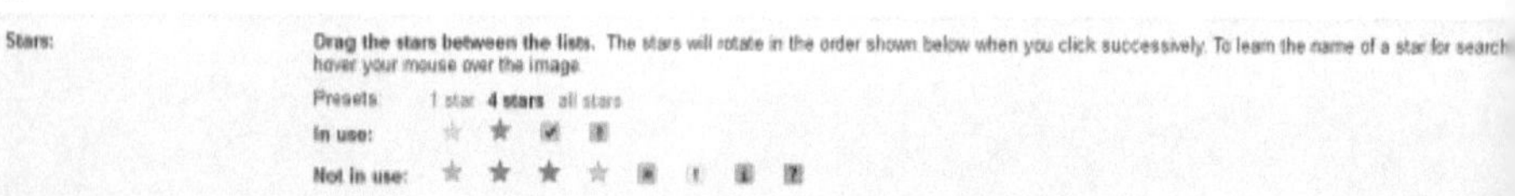

And by selecting all stars link you will be able to use all the stars

If you want don't want to use the presets , you can drag and drop which ever star you want to use by clicking and holding and left mouse button and pulling the star symbol from not in use to in use.

Note: you can only drag the stars one by one.

You can also drag the stars from in use to not in use for removing the stars from use; you can move it again whenever you want.

You can also re arrange the order of the stars in the in use list so that you can control which star appears first when you click the star symbol near the email message

Each star has a meaning. The stars are named after their color

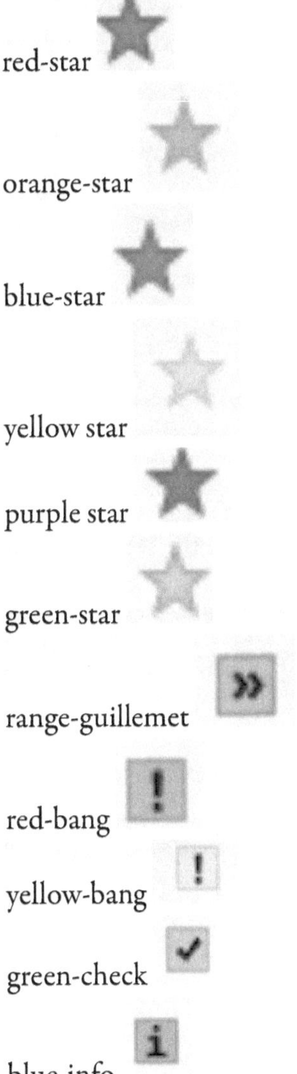

red-star

orange-star

blue-star

yellow star

purple star

green-star

range-guillemet

red-bang

yellow-bang

green-check

blue-info

purple-question

You can always hover your mouse over the symbol to know its name; I just made it a bit easy for you by giving a list above.

Now you can star your emails with appropriate stars and find it more easily.

After dragging all the stars you need into in use list, scroll down and click save changes button so you can use them.

You can click on the star symbol near your email message in your inbox, a star will be applied. To change the star you click again to choose a different star, click again and again to change the symbol.

I have starred a couple of emails for the purpose of demonstration.

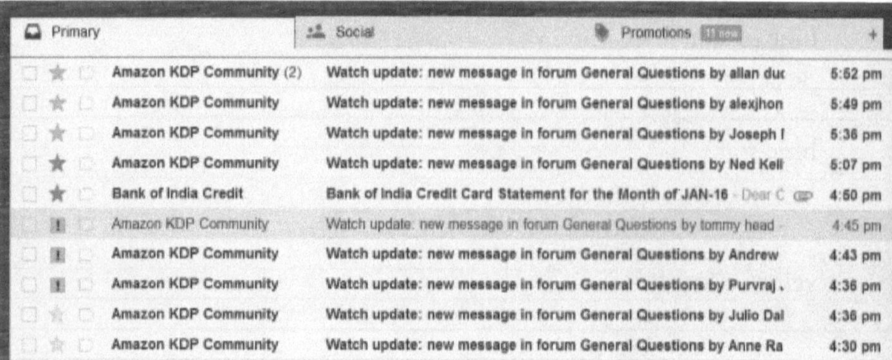

In the search bar above, I type has:blue-star and click the search button see the result in the image below.

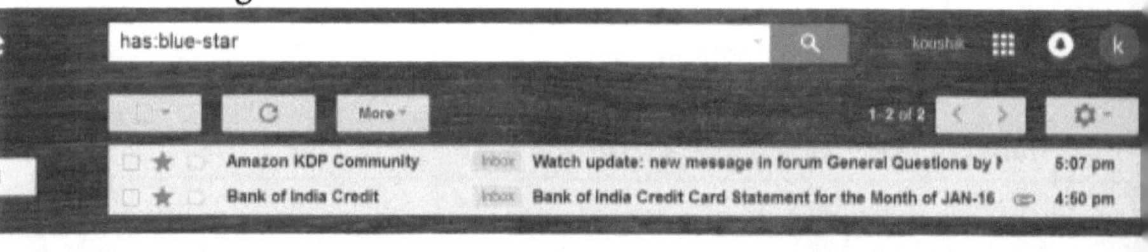

Search result for has:red-bang

Now you know how to use the has: keyword to search the starred messages

You can also scroll down the navigation slide bar in the left to find the link starred. Click that to see all your starred mail.

Note you can also remove the star by clicking the symbol of the starred message.

Using filters for automating your Gmail

Gmail's filters allow you to manage the flow of incoming messages. Using filters, you can automatically send email to a label, archive, delete, star, or forward your mail, even keep it out of Spam.

Click the small down arrow near the search bar

The search options will pop up and you can create an advanced search query using it

You can create different kinds of filters using different search queries.

Let me explain you about creating filters with a few examples

Example 1:

I want to label all the emails I receive from a particular email address and then archive it

Say I want to label all the email I receive from <kdp-no-reply@amazon.com> as amazon kdp and archive the emails

I enter kdp-no-reply@amazon.com in the from text box in the search options and click **create filter with this search** link

I click the skip the inbox checkbox

I click the mark as read checkbox

I click apply the label checkbox and select amazon kdp from the list of labels (I already created) I assume you already know how to create labels by now.

Then I click Also apply filter to ______matching conversations

What this does is it applies the filter to all emails which are already present and to all future emails matching this query.

I click the create filter button

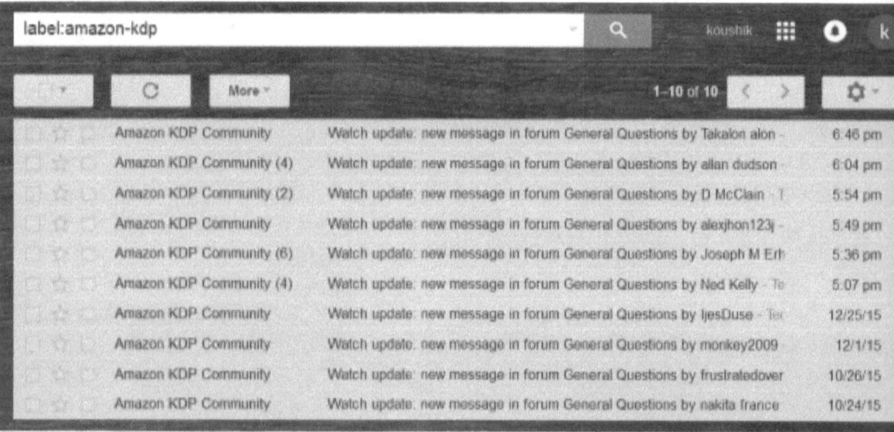

Now I don't see any email from kdp-no-reply@amazon.com in my inbox

I check the label amazon kdp and I find all the emails labelled and also marked as read

Now you know to create a basic filter, what if you want to remove your filter

Click the gear icon and then click settings

Click Filters and Blocked Addresses tab which is the fifth tab from the left

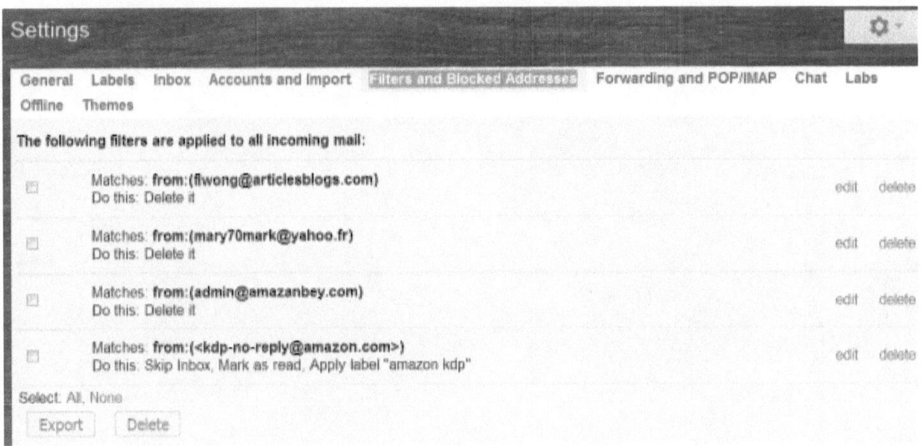

You see the list of all filters you may edit it or delete it; edit link takes you to the same search query page where you can edit the query

If you Click the delete link, a confirm delete filter pop up appears with yes and no buttons

Click the yes button to delete the filter

Note: the actions the filter already performed will not be changed. It is only that the filter won't be functioning in the future.

In this example, even if I have deleted the filter now I will still have emails in the amazon kdp label,

If I want it to be performed again I should create a filter again. (Because I have deleted the filter)

Another easy way to create a filter is to open an email or select an email by clicking the corresponding checkbox and then click more menu and then click Filter messages like these (see the image below)

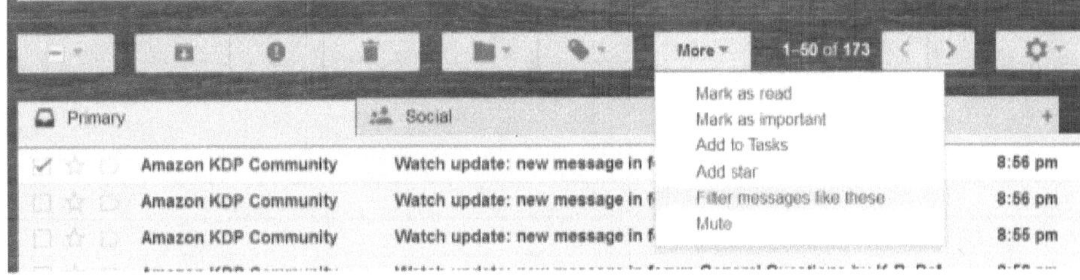

You will be taken to the search query with the from address of the email already entered.

The rest of the method is the same, verify the above example

Example 2:

In this example we will see how to forward certain emails with the help of filters.

But first you have to **add a forwarding email address**

Click the gear icon and select settings

Then click Forwarding and POP/IMAP link

Click add a forwarding address button

Enter the email address to which you want to forward the emails to and then click next

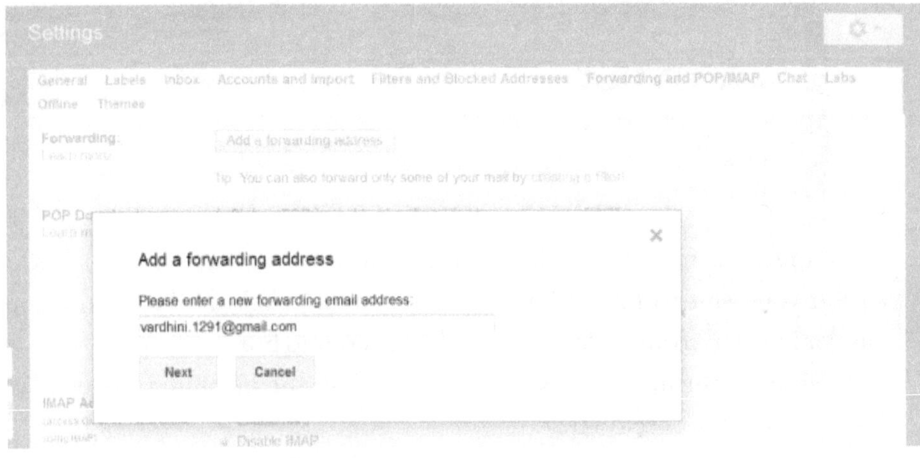

A popup window appears asking you to confirm

A confirmation code will be sent to the email address which you entered as a forwarding address. Let's say it's your business partner's email address

Now your partner should confirm by clicking a link from his/her email. This is done by Gmail to prevent spam. You contact your friend / business partner and ask him to confirm by clicking the link sent by Gmail.

Or if you are using this to forward the emails of this Gmail account to some of your own email addresses you should confirm by logging in to that email account clicking the confirmation link Gmail has sent you.

You click ok and wait for your partner to confirm or go to your other email address and click the confirmation link

Now after your business partner has confirmed and permitted you to forward emails.

Go back to Forwarding and POP/IMAP tab of your Gmail settings

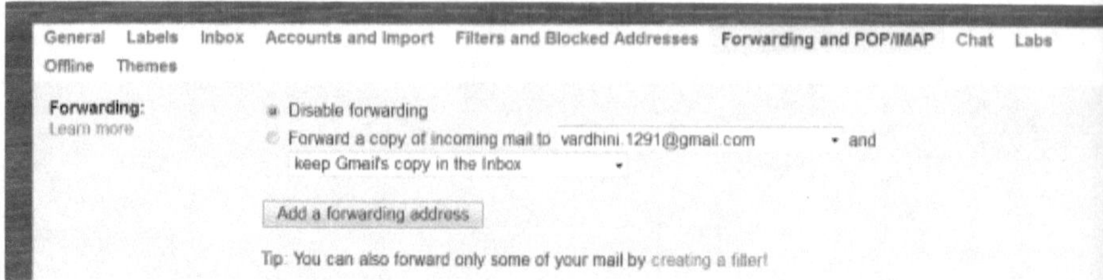

Your page will look similar to the screenshot shown above

If you want to forward all incoming emails, click the Forward a copy of incoming mail to and select the email from combo box.

Mostly your intention is not to forward all the incoming email so we are going to use filters to do that.

Note: You can also add multiple emails following the same method as forwarding addresses and forward different kinds of emails you receive to different email addresses using filters.

Say I want to forward all emails from kdp-no-reply@amazon.com I open an email sent to me by that email address

Then click more and select filter messages like these

Then a search options page appears with kdp-no-reply@amazon.com in the from text box

Click create filter with this search link

Then select forward it to checkbox and select that friend's email address from the combo box

(See image below)

Also apply filter to 2 matching conversations and click create filter button from:(kdp-no-reply@amazon.com)

« back to search options

When a message arrives that matches this search:

☐ Skip the Inbox (Archive it)

☐ Mark as read

☐ Star it

☐ Apply the label: Choose label... ⬍

☑ Forward it to: vardhini.1291@gmail.com

☐ Delete it

☐ Never send it to Spam

☐ Always mark it as important

☐ Never mark it as important

☐ Categorize as: Choose category... ⬍

Create filter   ☑ Also apply filter to **2** matching conversations.

Learn more
Note: old mail will not be forwarded

Now you have learned the powerful feature of filters. You can add multiple email addresses and forward to them different kinds of emails using filters.

You can also select the delete it checkbox so that the forwarded emails would be deleted automatically.

You can do many things with filters. There are limitless possibilities of automation like forwarding and labelling. You can reduce a lot of manual work and save your time.

Now let me tell you about the other options in create filter page

We have already discussed archive, label, and forwarding emails through filters and also deleting emails through filters

Star it: stars all emails matching your search query

Never send it to spam: Gmail doesn't send it to spam, the emails matching your search query

Always mark as important: marks the emails matching your query as important

Always mark as important: never marks the emails matching the search query as important

Categorize as: categorize the emails matching your query in to primary, social, promotions, forums or updates according to your choice.

Now you know about creating filters, let us create complex filters with advanced search queries in the next chapter.

Creating Advanced filters using complex search queries

Let me teach how to create filters to deal with multiple senders email addresses.

Say if you want to label all your close friends' email as best friends automatically. You can create a filter with multiple email addresses in your from: text box using the **OR keyword**

Click the small down arrow near the search box

The search option page appears

Enter multiple emails which you may wish to handle in the format shown below

Nam1@example.com OR name2@Gmail.com OR name3@example.om

Note the OR keyword should be in capital letters. (See image below)

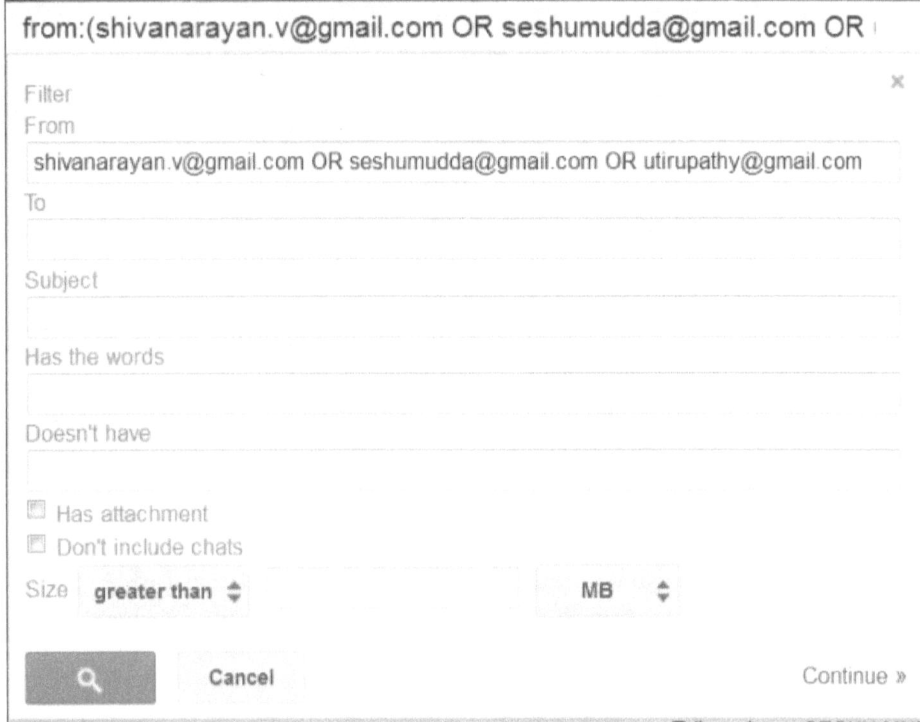

After entering all the email addresses you would like to use the filter on, click create filter with this search link

Create filter page appears, now whatever you do using this filter will be applied any email address you typed in from: text box

I want to label all the emails I receive from my best friends as frnds

So I click apply the label checkbox and select frnds from the combo box

Then I click Also apply filter to matching conversations. Check box and click Create filter button

This time I did not archive the emails so I find them in inbox also with the label frnds in it

Now I go to labels list in navigation slide bar and click frnds label

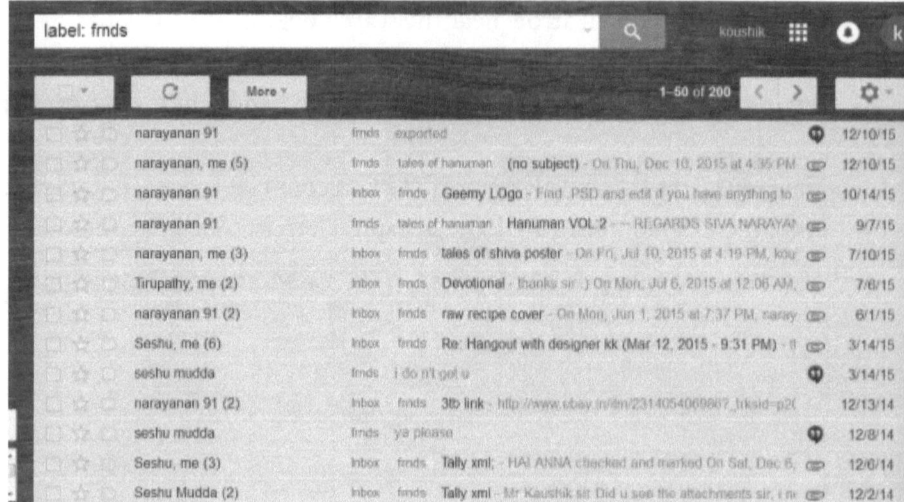

Has these words

Has keyword is used to search for words in the email this is very useful in creating search queries

I want to create a filter to star all emails that has the word payment. To do that I must

Click the down arrow near search bar

In has the words text box, type payment

Here we can also use multiple inputs using the OR keyword for example

I enter payment OR payments OR PayPal

Click create filter with this search

Click the star it checkbox

Click Also apply filter to matching conversations checkbox

Click create filter

Then I click starred side navigation slide-bar and there are many starred emails which contains the word payment or PayPal

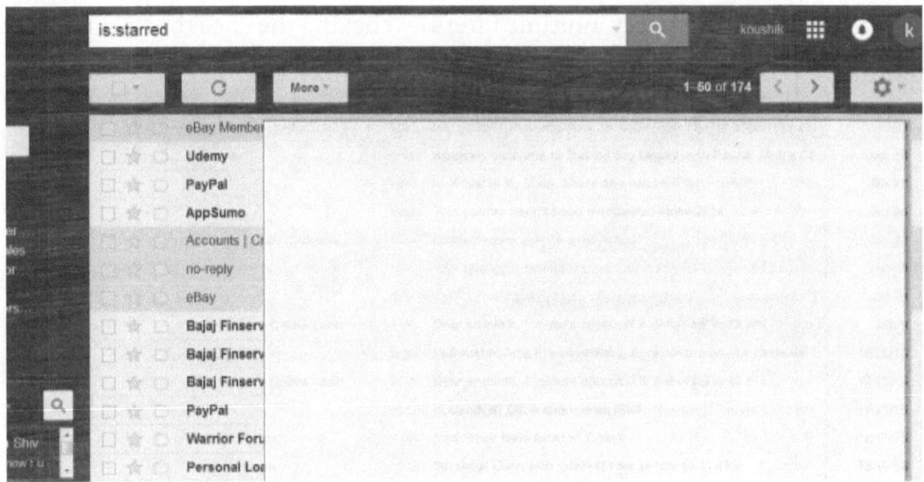

I don't find the result useful so I want to edit this filter

Editing a filter

Click the gear icon and then click settings

Click Filters and Blocked Addresses

You will see the list of filters you have already created

Click the edit link near the filter which you would like to edit

In the above example, I have typed the words payment OR payment OR PayPal in the has these words text box and I said that I am not satisfied with the result I got. Let me change it now

I am going to delete what I typed in has these words textbox and I am going to type the same words payment OR payments OR PayPal in subject text box.

While editing a filter you will see a continue link instead of create filter with this search link

Click that continue link

I still want it to be starred so I am not editing the filter page, you will find update filter button. Click it and now your filter is updated.

Deleting a filter

Click the gear icon and then click settings

Click Filters and Blocked Addresses

You will see the list of filters you have already created

Click the delete link near the filter which you would like to delete

You can also select multiple filters by clicking the checkbox near the filter
After selecting the filters you want to delete, press the delete button

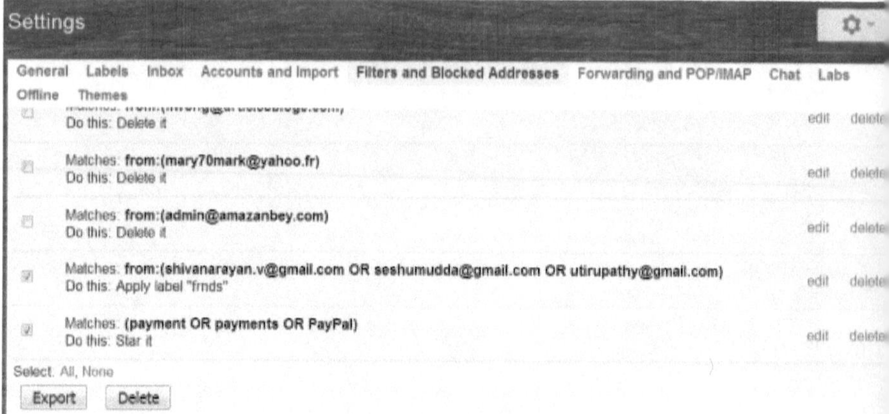

When you press the delete button, confirm delete filter dialog box will
popup click ok and the selected filters will be deleted.

Gear Icon settings

Let's explore the settings in the gear Icon

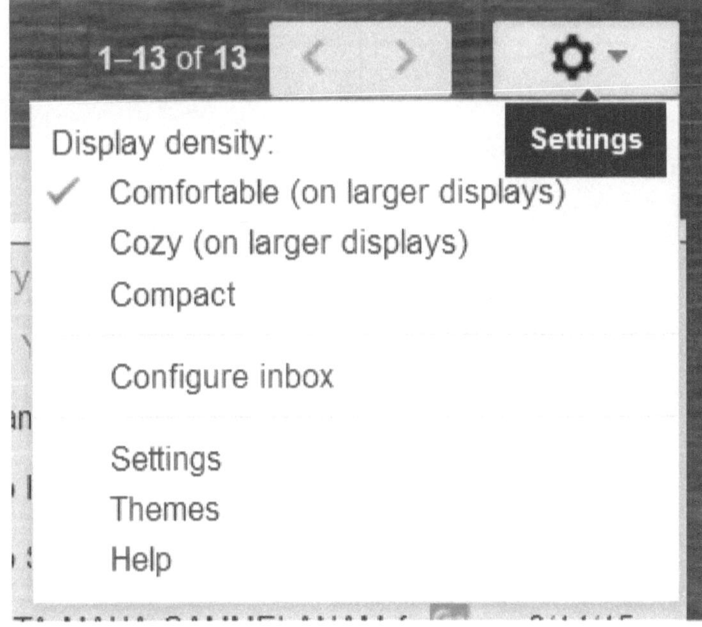

What is display density?

It is basically the space adjustment between emails in your message box. Please see the images below to see the different display density

The best way to choose is to select between the display density options and see it yourself which suits your need

To explain in simple words, comfortable is the density where your emails are spread out and is nice to view in broader screen settings

Compact display density lessens the space between emails in the message box

See the two views below to compare and understand.

Cozy is somewhere between comfortable and compact.

I always use compact because I like to see more number of emails in a single page.

19 PLUS TIPS FOR USING GMAIL TO THE FULLEST: GMAIL AUTOMATION AND USING THIRD PARTY TOOLS

Comfortable view

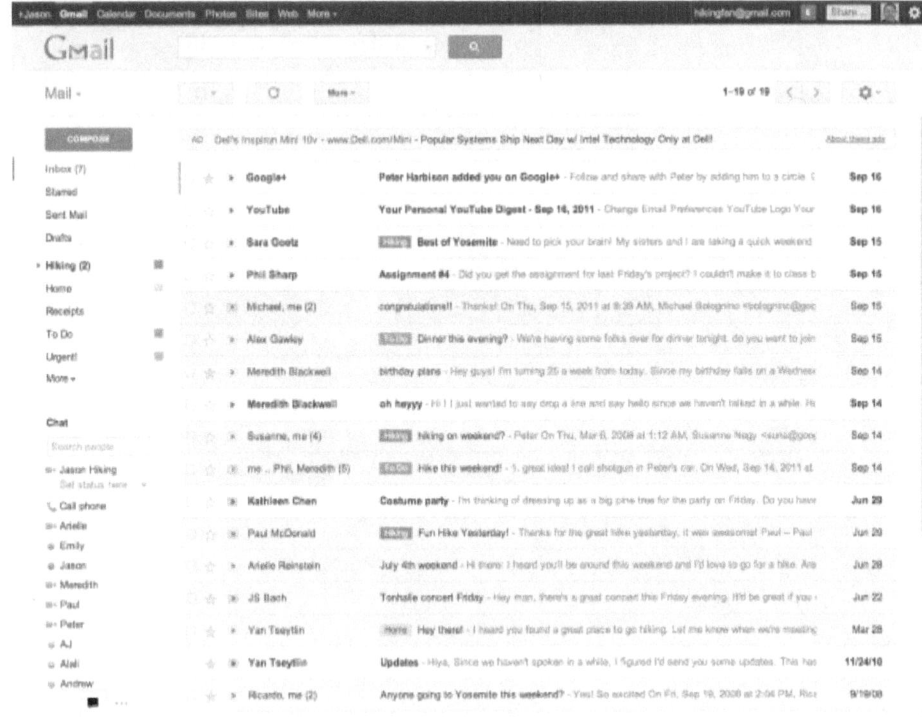

Compact view

Okay now there is small problem you may experience with these settings. If you don't have that problem then everything's fine,

If you experience being stuck in Gmail Compact mode, even if you change the display density settings (see image below)

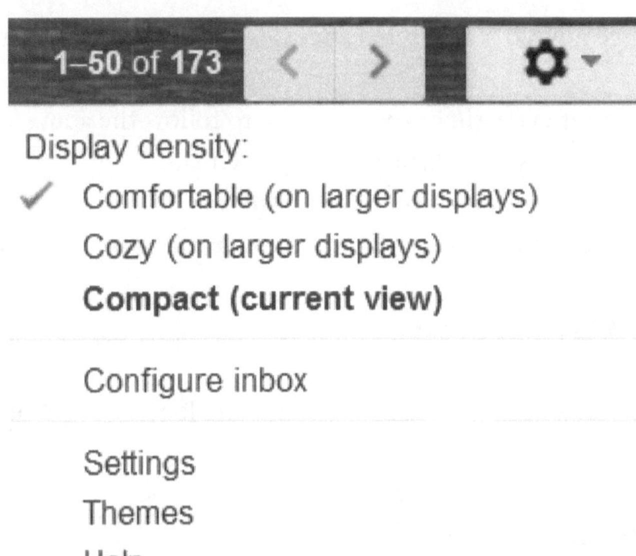

In the above image if you see, the comfortable is ticked but compact is in bold with current view in brackets. If you get this problem you can follow the below instructions to solve it.

STEP 1: clear your browsers history completely

Step 2: log in to your Gmail

Step 3: click the gear icon and select the display density you want

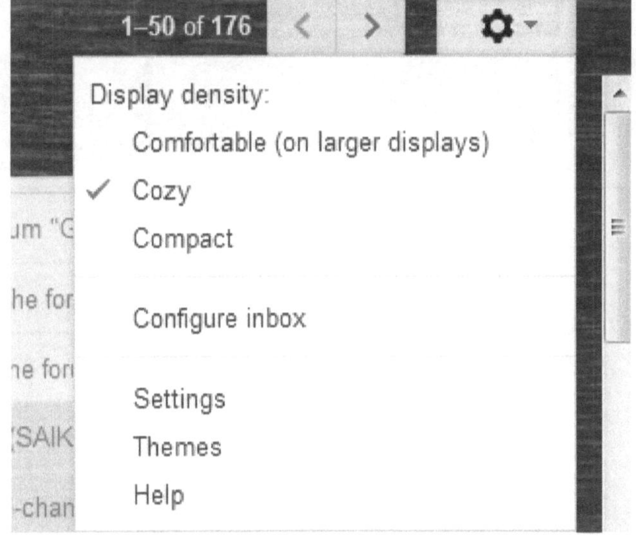

See the above image now cozy is selected after clearing my browsers history completely

You don't have to do it every time; you just have to follow the above steps when you are not able to change the display density of Gmail.

Note comfortable will work only on larger displays

We have already discussed about configure inbox in the gear icon. Refer here

Settings we will discuss in a separate chapter

Themes

Themes give us a collection of designs to change the look and feel of the Gmail

Click the gear icon and select themes

Pick a theme page will appear (see below)

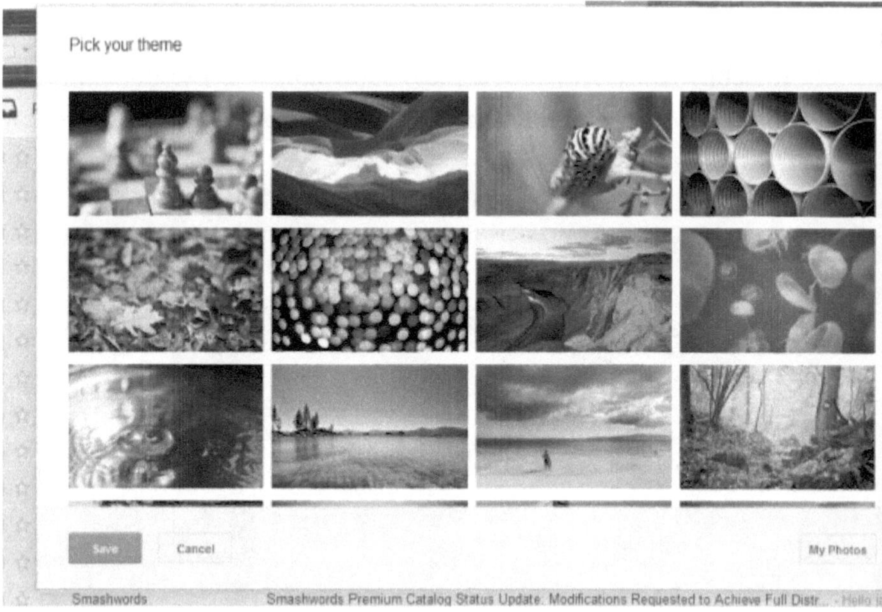

Select any theme you want and then click save

See Tree theme in my Gmail now

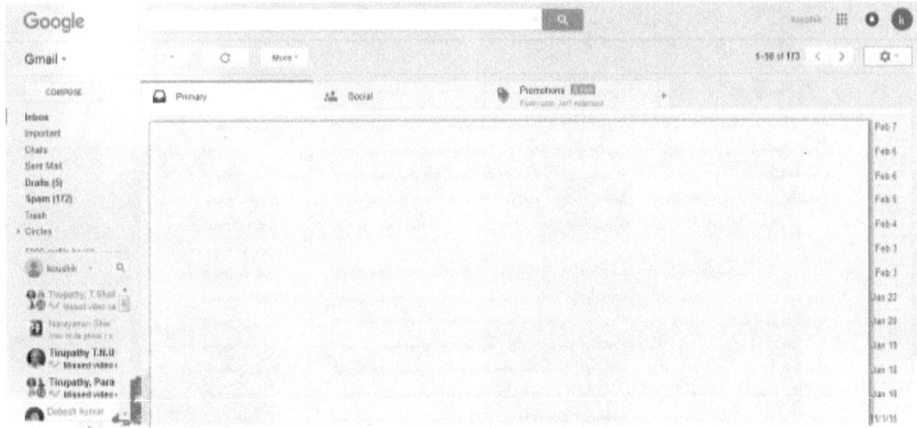

Do you know you can upload your pictures for themes?

Click the gear icon and select themes

Pick a theme page will appear

Click my photos in right corner in the bottom of the dialog box

The select your background image page will appear

With my photos as the selected tab. You will see all the photo albums you have, choose a photo and click select.

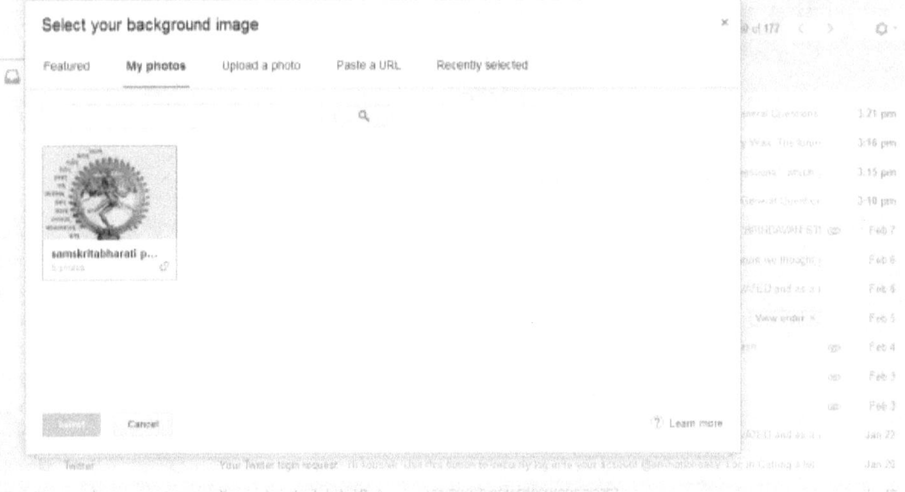

To select your background from the featured images you click featured tab and you can select any image from it by clicking it and then click the select button to apply it. The featured changes from time to time as new images are featured by Gmail

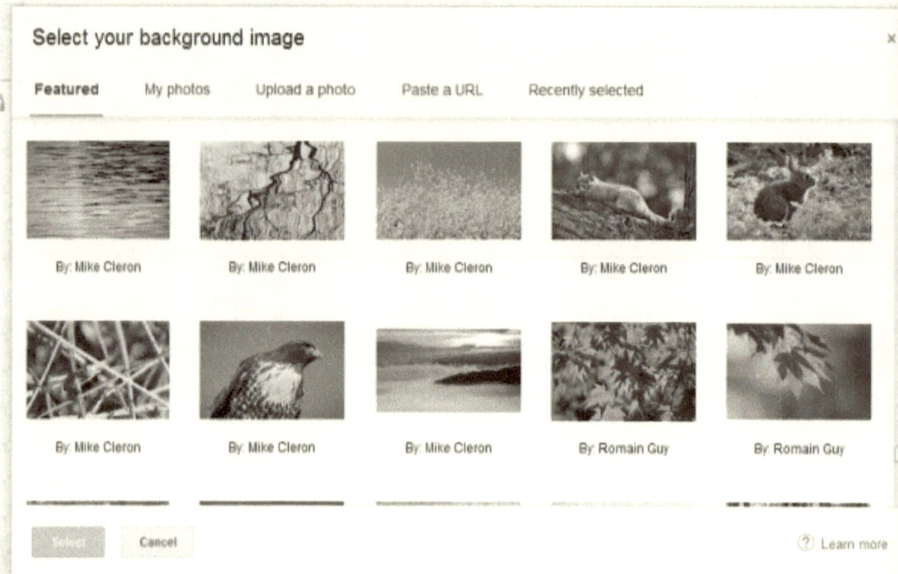

. To upload a photo, click upload a photo tab

Then drag a photo in to that page, or click select a photo from your computer button and then browse and upload any photo you want to.

Then wait for the image to be uploaded

Click save to pick the uploaded image as your theme

You can also find an image from the internet and paste that image URL and choose it as your theme

After finding your image from the internet and viewing the images. Copy the image's URL (link)

In your Gmail go to my photos Gear>themes>my photos (I told you in detail before)

Select the paste a URL tab

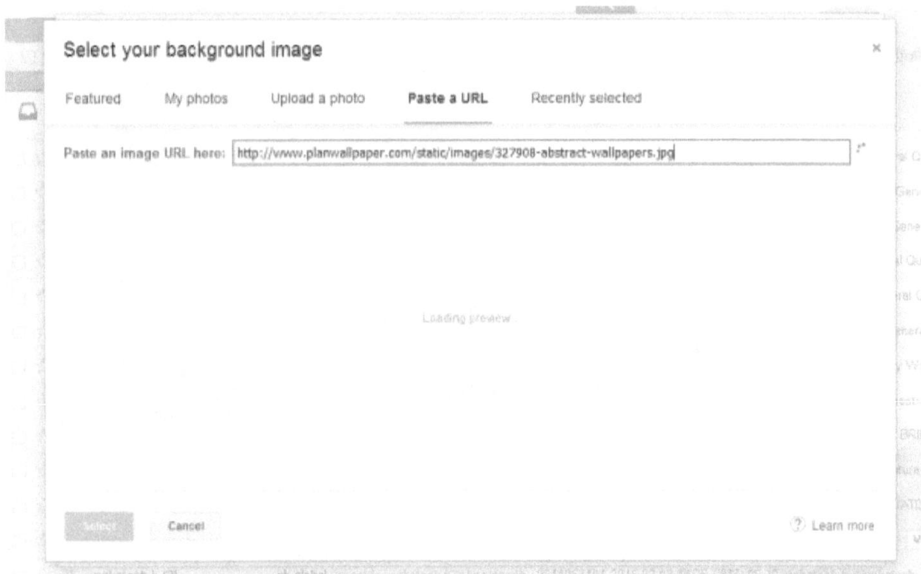

Paste the URL you copied in to the text box as shown above

After some seconds the page shows you the image preview

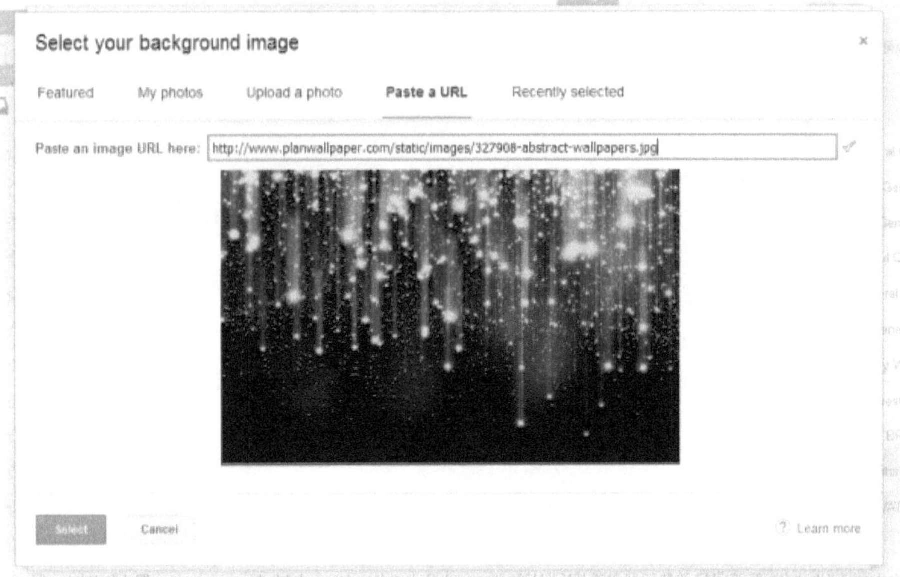

Click select. Another page appears now click save and now the image you found in the internet is your Gmail theme.

In the recently selected tab you can see all the themes; you can see all the images you used as themes recently.

Exploring your Gmail settings tab by tab

General tab

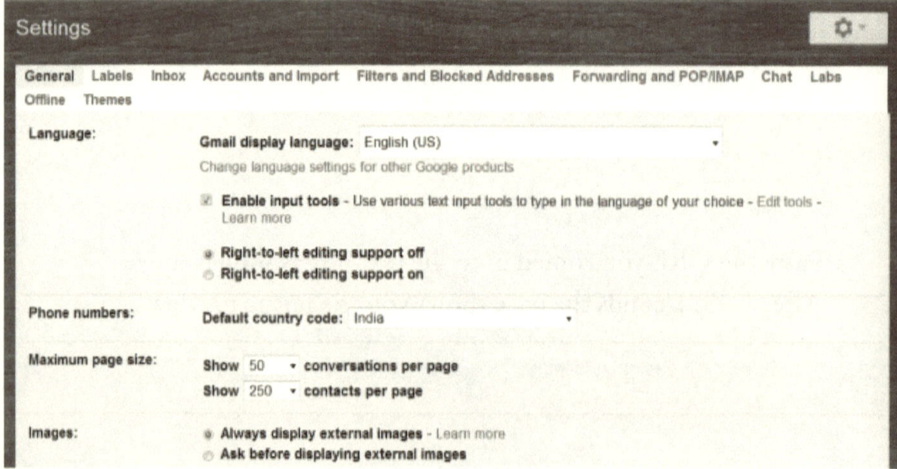

Click the gear icon and select settings by clicking it

The settings page will appear, the first tab of the settings page is general

In general tab of the settings page first option is the

Language, select a language from the Gmail display language combo box and all your menus and options will change to the selected language after you click save changes. Click the enable input tools checkbox if it is not ticked already. It is useful to type in various languages inside Gmail. I use this feature a lot.

If you are using a language that uses a right to left script, Urdu for example, you need to click tight to left editing support on. I don't use it, so I have my right to left editing support off selected.

Phone numbers select your country from the default country code combo box.

19 PLUS TIPS FOR USING GMAIL TO THE FULLEST: GMAIL AUTOMATION AND USING THIRD PARTY TOOLS

Maximum page size: in show __ conversations per page combo box you can select the number of email conversations to show in a single page the minimum you can select is 10 and maximum is 100 conversations

Contacts per page is the number of contacts you want Gmail to show you. You can select between 50, 100, and 250 from the dropdown box

Images has two options Always display external images

Always display external images

If Always display external images is selected, all the html emails and any emails containing embedded images, are automatically displayed with the images. This is useful if you love reading html email with all the cool images and you don't worry about images being loaded and displayed without your explicit concern.

Ask before displaying external images

This option is useful if you only want to read text emails and you would like to be asked if you want the images of the particular email is to be loaded and displayed or not. This always saves your internet usage if you have a data limit, this option comes in very handy for you.

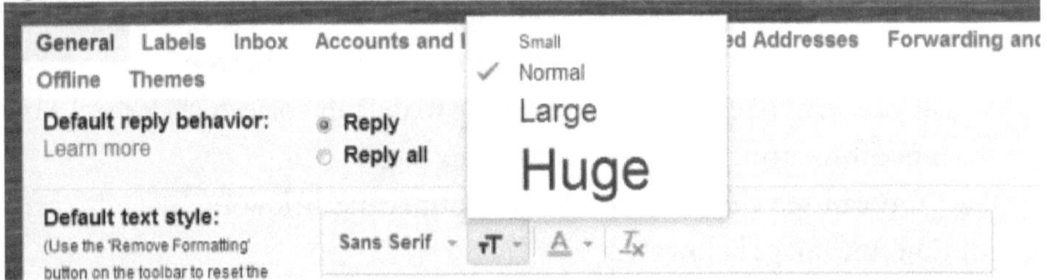

Default reply behaviour: you can choose reply or reply all. This determines what happens when you click the reply in your email conversations.

Default text styles

This is used to set the default font, text size, text colour etc in all the emails you send.

In case you want to remove the formatting which was set through your settings page for a particular email you are sending, you can always use the remove formatting button in your new message page or reply page see image below.

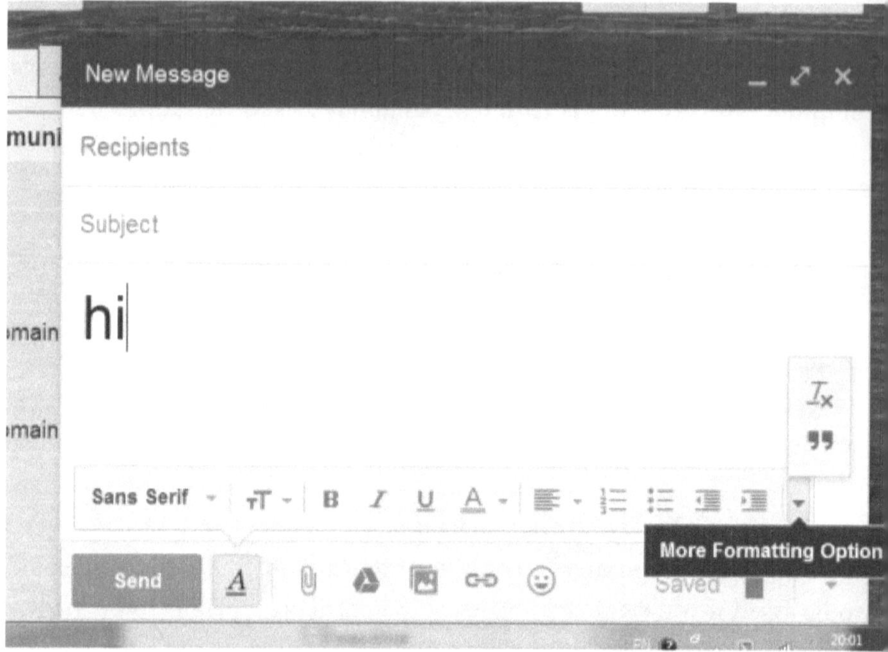

Click the formatting button A (highlighted in the above image)

Then the formatting toolbar will appear, click the down arrow button and then select Tx button which is the remove formatting button.

If you want to change the formatting to default you can click the Tx button (remove formatting button) in the setting page.

You can see the preview of your formatting below the default text style option (see image below)

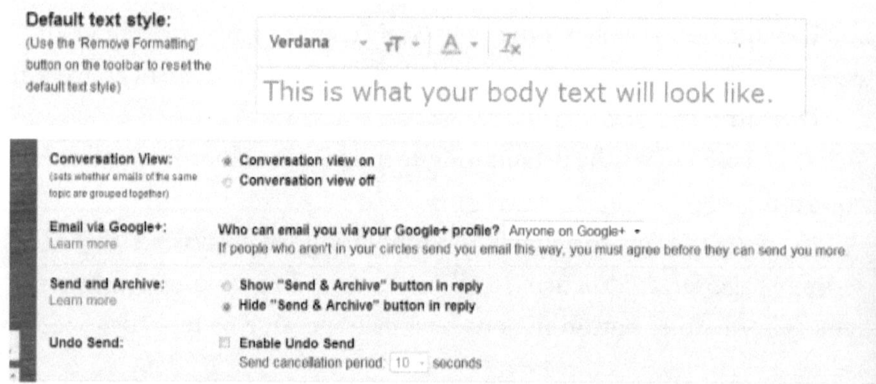

Conversations view: there are two options here, **Conversations view on and Conversations view off.** If conversation view on is selected, all the related conversations are clustered together and if conversation view off is selected, your inbox only contains the emails sent to you.

There are advantages of conversation view and sometimes disadvantages too.

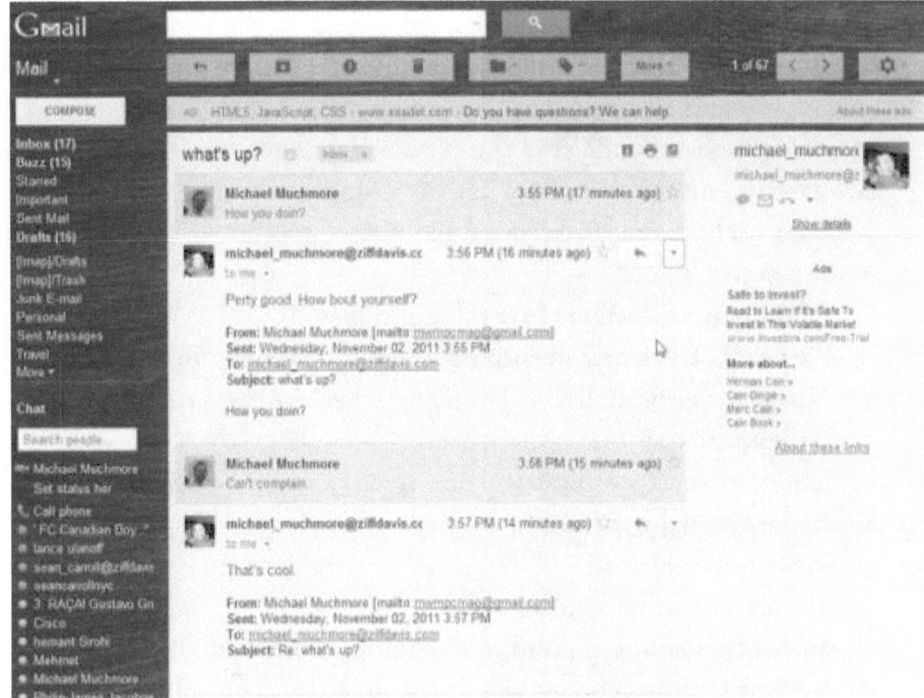

By default, Gmail displays all back-and-forth replies along with the original message, with their subject lines stacked to create what they call a conversation view. It can be an efficient way to see related emails all in one place or it can make for a confusing on-screen display.

The advantages are: you can see the replies you have sent and the replies you have received relating to a subject very easily.

The disadvantages are: when email conversations involve multiple email addresses, sometimes conversations look messy so you have to play around and choose which is better for you.

Email via Google+: you can select who can email you through Google plus, you can select the options from the combo box, the options are anyone on Google plus, Extended circles, circles, no one.

Send and archive: has two options, Show "Send & Archive" button in reply and Hide "Send & Archive" button in reply. If you like archiving all the emails you sent reply to, send and archive button will be very useful to you. If you don't do that, you can select hide because that button is not necessary to you.

Undo Send: sometimes you may want to undo a sent email, if you sent something by accident and you want to correct it, you can do that now but only if you have sent the email just now and you want to undo it, for up to 30 seconds you have time and then you cannot undo.

Tick the enable undo send checkbox and in send cancellation period drop down menu, you can select from 5 to 30 seconds.

Stars we have already discussed about stars in detail. In a previous chapter so you can refer there.

Desktop notifications: have three options

First click "Click here to enable desktop notifications for Gmail" Link

New mail notifications on - Notify me when any new message arrives in my inbox or primary tab

Important mail notifications on - Notify me only when an important message arrives in my inbox

Mail notifications off

The options are self explanatory.

You will get notifications to your desktop according to the selected option.

Keyboard shortcuts: we will discuss it in a separate chapter please refer here

Button labels: you can choose between icons and text, I like icons, you may like them too if not you can choose text, when we choose icons, we can always hover over the icons and find what that icon is for from the tooltips. For me, icons look neater than text.

My picture: to add your picture,

Select a picture link then a new page pops up

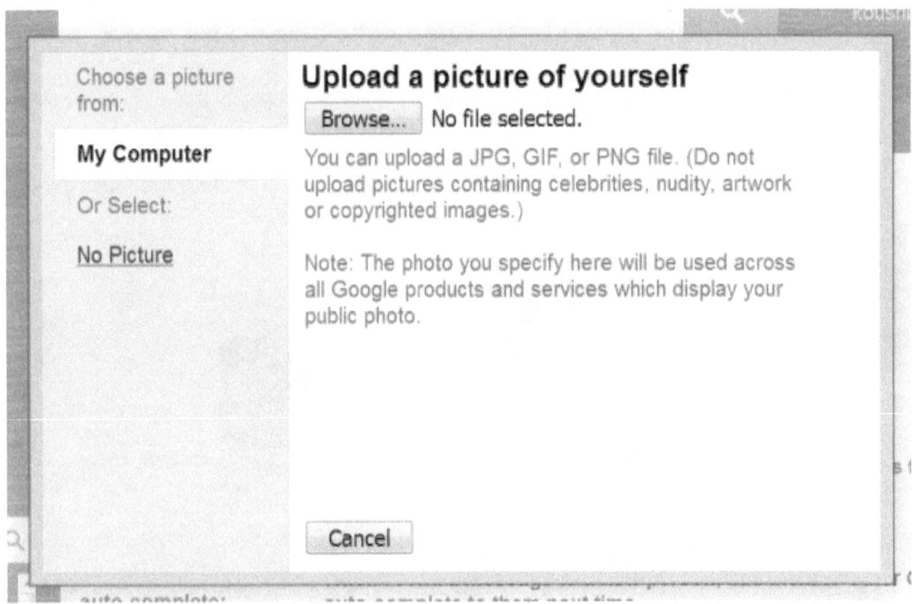

Click browse

Select a picture from your desktop and click open, it will show uploading image (see below)

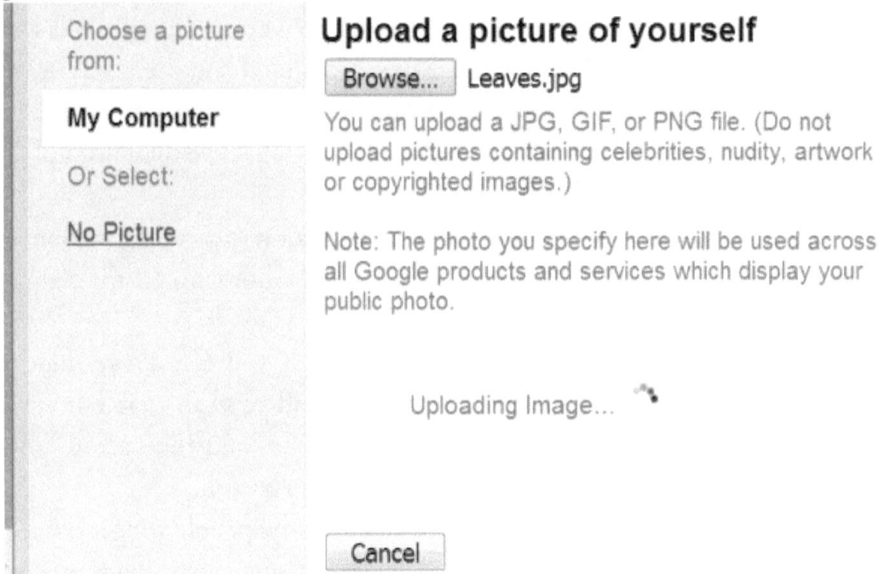

Please wait for it to upload. Then you will see crop this picture of yourself page,

Just move that square by clicking and holding the left mouse button and moving the mouse. See the preview box.

After adjusting the box by moving the square, click apply changes. Your picture is successfully uploaded and everyone to whom you reply will see that image. You can also upload an avatar or something if you don't want to show your real photo but uploading your real photo and showing that to your clients and customers or even family and friends is more effective than just uploading avatars.

People widget: The **People** widget of Gmail displays information about your contacts (contact name, email address...). It shows up on the right hand side of your Gmail layout in your conversation.

It's useful sometimes but if you don't use it you can always hide it by clicking hide the people widget radio-button and you can enable it any time you want by clicking gear icon > settings>general and then scroll down to people widget and click show people widget radio button.

Now it's natural for you to get a doubt, I see the people widget has a lot of details for some people and for others it doesn't show anything except name. Why is it so? I also got this doubt when I started using it.

All you have to do is edit the contact details you have about that particular person let me explain you with screenshots.

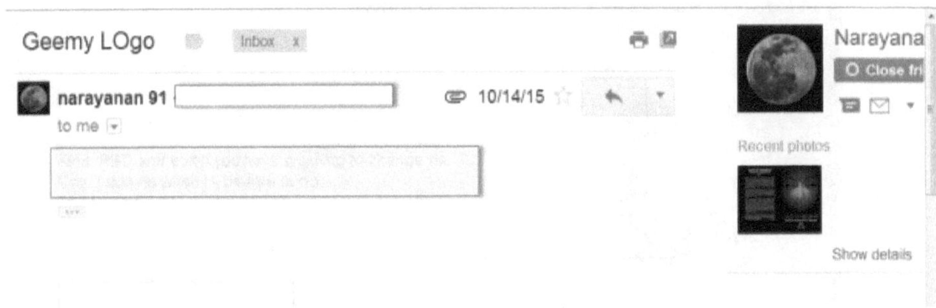

See the above image my friends people widget shows he is a close friend in Google plus and a link to hangout and email.

Google contacts preview will open

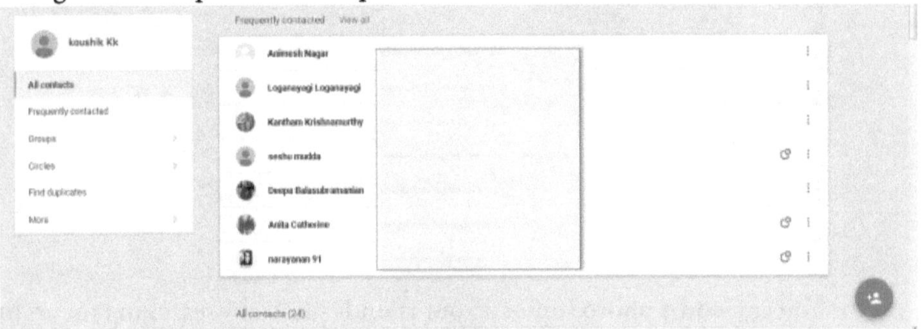

Hover your mouse pointer over the contact you want to edit, and then click the pencil icon to edit the contact

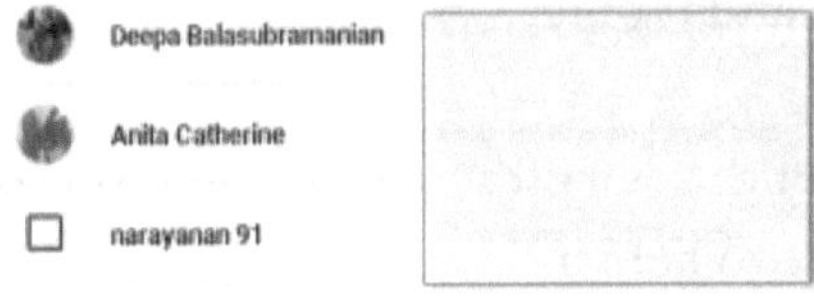

Edit contact page will pop up

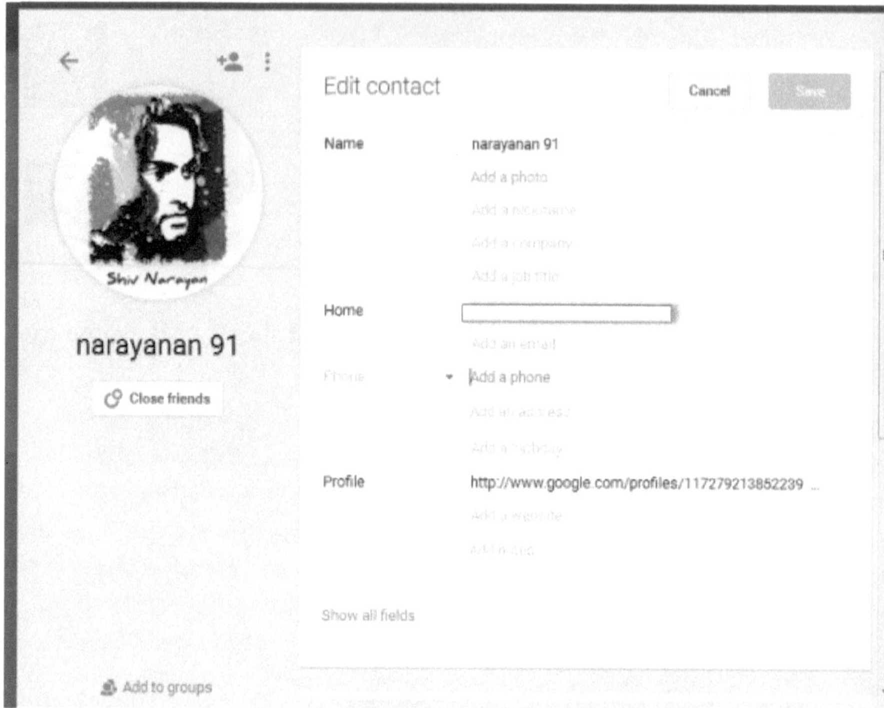

You can add a photo (upload your friends photo by searching for an image from your pc and upload it is very similar like you uploaded the photos for theme. So I am not explaining it again. A nick name, a company a job title and phone number etc just by clicking there and typing.

After everything is done, click save.

Create contacts for auto-complete: this is a great option, I am too lazy to add contacts myself, I use Gmail's feature to help me.

Click "When I send a message to a new person, add them to Other Contacts so that I can auto-complete to them next time" radio button.

If you like adding contacts by yourself, click "I'll add contacts myself" radio button

Importance signals for ads: using this you can select what type of ads you love to see. You already know that Gmail is going to show ads to you. Why not choose what you like, at least this gives you some control over what you see. Google will serve you with better and relevant ads. It's a win-win right!

To change those ad preferences, click the "here" link and a new tab will open.

19 PLUS TIPS FOR USING GMAIL TO THE FULLEST: GMAIL AUTOMATION AND USING THIRD PARTY TOOLS

You can check or uncheck the checkboxes by clicking, you can click add new interest and start typing, the form will show you options as you type (see image below)

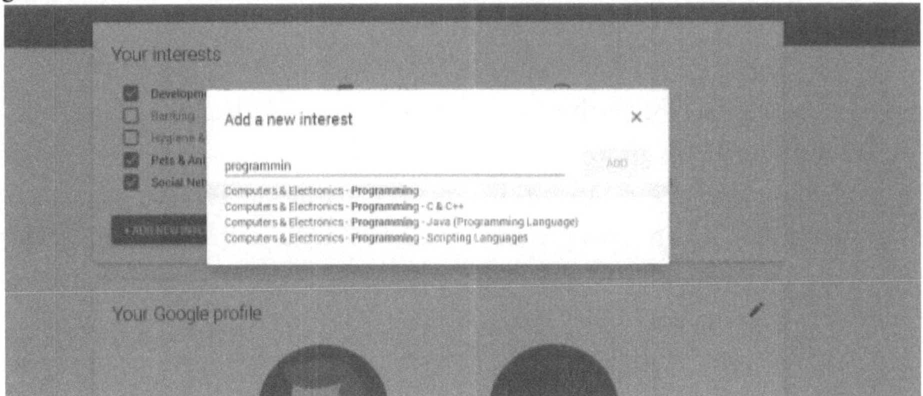

Then click the options shown and then click add

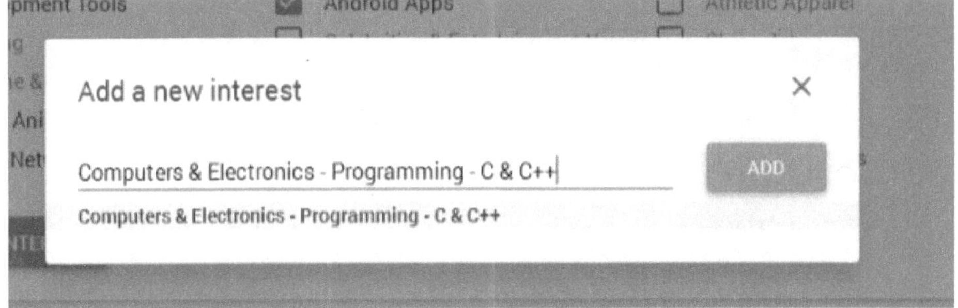

Scroll down
You will see this

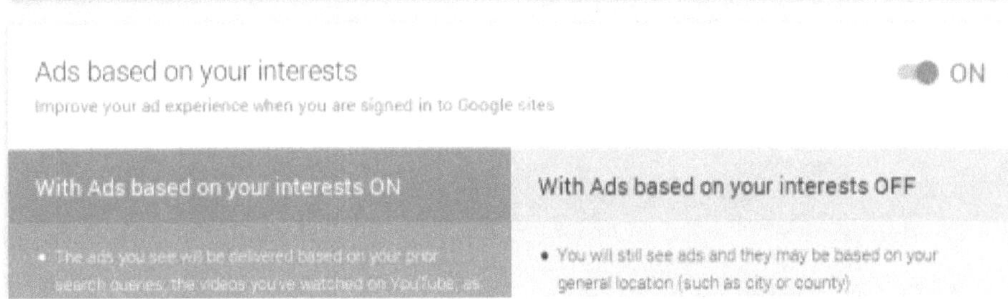

You can click the green on to turn it off, but I suggest you not to do that. You can read the benefits of leaving it on that page. In my opinion there is nothing more to play around with in that page, let's close the page and get back to our Gmail account.

I remind you, we are in the general tab of the settings page. Let's continue exploring the options present there.

Signature: you can design a good signature with images and links let's do that

It's just like writing in your email compose page or reply page

Use the text formatting options, use the insert link and insert images icon etc, you can play with it.

You can also use Insert this signature before quoted text in replies and remove the "—" line that precedes it. Checkbox so your signature is in the top of the quoted message in replies so people could see your signature standing out in the long emails

Indicators: personally I don't use indicators but you can use it if you find it helpful in differentiating the emails.

To use it click Show indicators radio button.

Preview of indicators below

Displays an arrow (›) by messages sent to my address (not a mailing list)

Display of double arrow (») by messages sent only to me.

Snippets: I use snippets because it's easy and very useful to find what the email message is really about. It's better to know what's inside without opening an email. Right?

Click show snippets radio button to enable it and no snippets radio button to disable it.

Vacation responder: this is very useful for professionals and business people. We can use a vacation responder when we are in a vacation. But more importantly we can use them at work. sending an automatic reply saying I have received you email and I will respond you shortly is a good thing if you are a business person, freelancer or any kind of person dealing with customers, buyers, clients etc. It definitely gives a professional look.

To do this, set the first day to the current date and you don't have to give a last date.

Type in a subject and message

You can click only send a response to people in my Contacts checkbox but for me it is not relevant I want all the people who email me to get an acknowledgement from me.

Click save changes.

Note: In fact it is better for you to click save changes immediately after editing a setting so you don't forget to click it at last.

Labels Tab

The next tab of the settings page is labels let's have a glance.

There is really nothing much to do with the labels tab

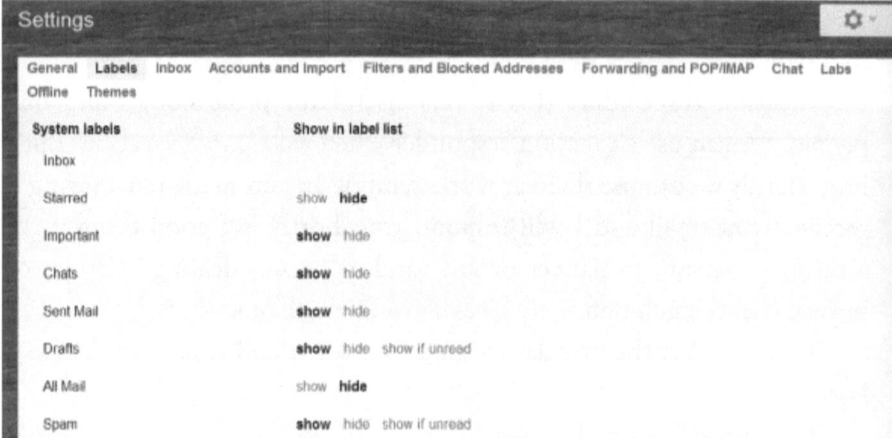

It lists all the system labels

System labels are the labels created by Gmail by default, they are inbox, starred, important, chats, sent mail, drafts, all mail, spam, and thrash

Gmail gives you options whether to show these labels or hide them,

You cannot hide the inbox, which is obvious.

For drafts and spam you have another option show if unread, by clicking this you will see the label only if there are unread messages in it. If you have opened all the emails in that label that label hides automatically and it shows when something new appears inside the label.

Below all the system labels the categories are listed.

With show and hide options in both Show in message list and show in labels list

19 PLUS TIPS FOR USING GMAIL TO THE FULLEST: GMAIL AUTOMATION AND USING THIRD PARTY TOOLS

By now you know what a labels list is.

What is a message list?

Message list is the list of messages in any view of Gmail. By show and hide in message list you can control whether the label is shown in the left side of the message.

Then there is circles listed with the same options such as categories.

Then comes the labels

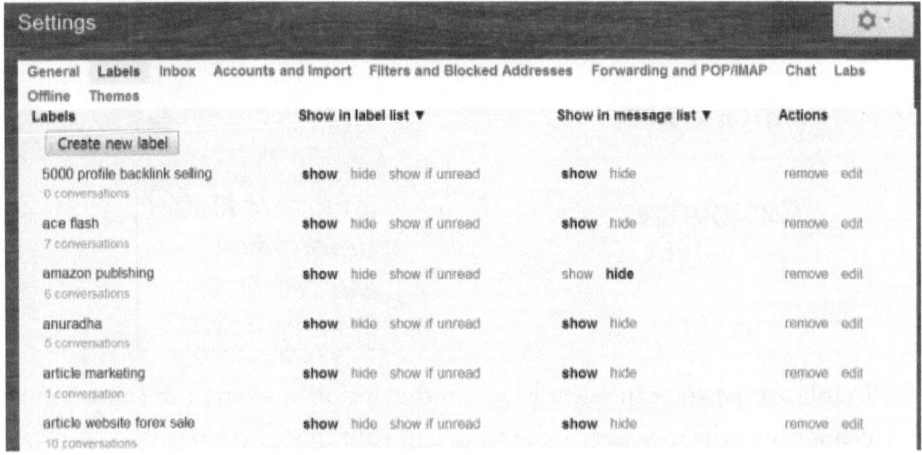

You can use the create new label button to create a label, the steps to create a label is the same as you learned before.

Every label has a label name listed and shows how many conversations are labelled under that particular label.

All the labels have the options show, hide and show if unread, we discussed these options just now, and then there is remove and edit,

Remove: by clicking remove a remove label dialog box will pop up. Click delete to get it removed.

Edit: by clicking edit label pops up and you can change the label name there and also the parent category if you want. Then click save.

Note: Removing a label will not remove the messages with that label.

Inbox Tab

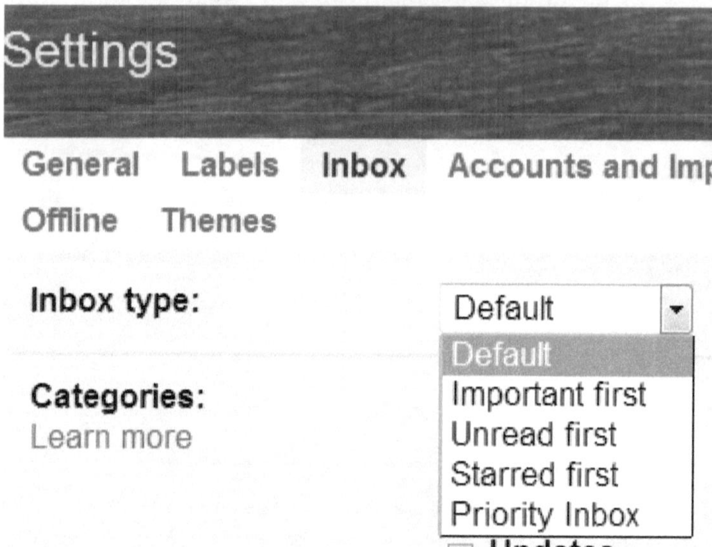

In inbox type you can select between the options shown in the above image to change how the messages are arranged in your inbox.

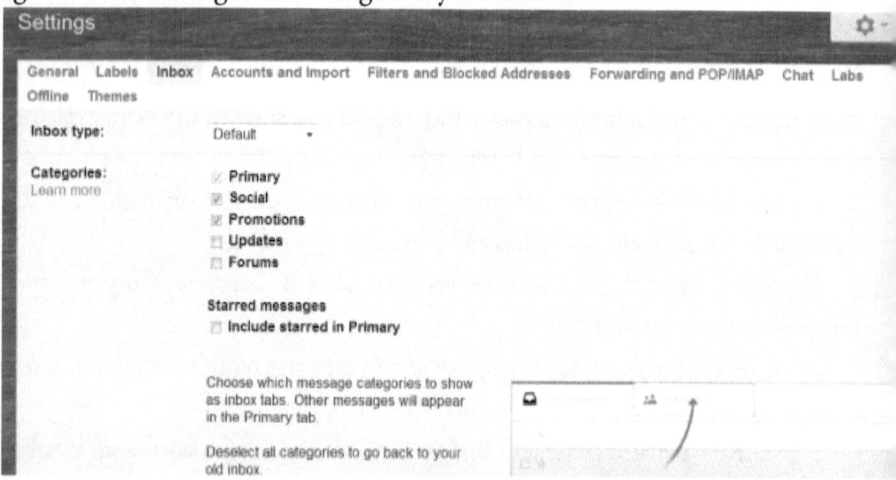

Categories we already discussed before. You can select what categories you want from this page also.

Selecting show markers will show that yellow arrow in the left of your messages which are marked as important.

Clicking no markers will hide that yellow arrow.

Clicking the Use my past actions to predict which messages are important to me. Radio button will instruct Gmail to analyze your past actions with those types of emails to predict which emails are important.

If you don't want Gmail to do so you can click "don't use my past actions to predict which messages are important". But anyhow there will always be an important list and Gmail is not going to stop marking emails as important, at least for now.

So in my opinion, it's better to instruct Gmail to predict using past actions so my important emails are accurate.

Filtered emails: sometimes you may receive emails which Gmail thinks is important, but your filter moves it out of inbox. Gmail asks you whether to follow the filter's instructions (filter is created by you) or Gmail's analysis

I don't like to override filters because filters are manually created by us and important marking is Gmail's prediction.

Now click save changes.

Accounts and Import Tab

In this tab we will configure to maintain multiple email accounts using Gmail, change password and security settings and also import contacts from other emails, etc

Change account settings:

Change password: click the change password link and a new window will open, you will be asked to login by entering your email address and password and click sign in

Password page will open, you can enter new password confirm it by re-entering the new password and click change password button.

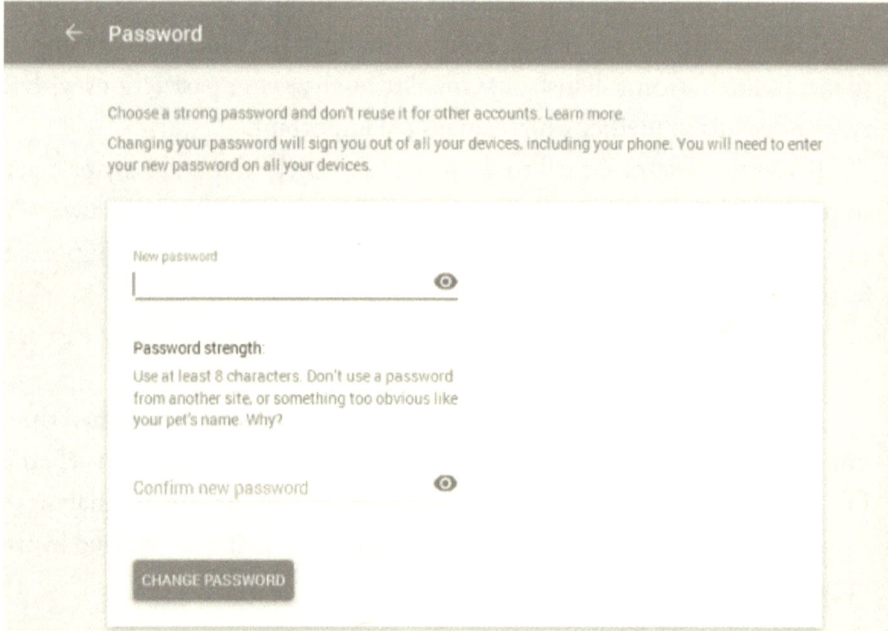

Change password recovery options: click Change password recovery options link, sign in and security page will open.

It will show when you last changed your password.

Below that you can turn on two-step verification by clicking the on/off toggle switch

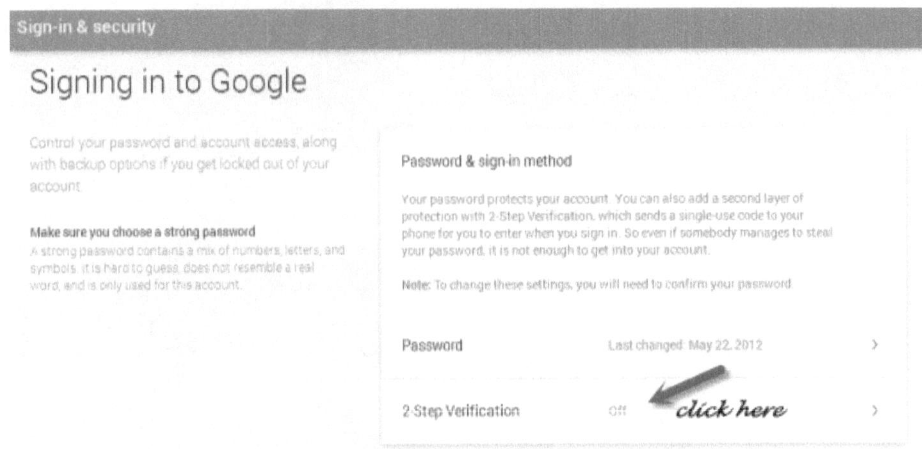

A new page will open click the start setup button

Then enter your phone number and click text message radio button and click send code

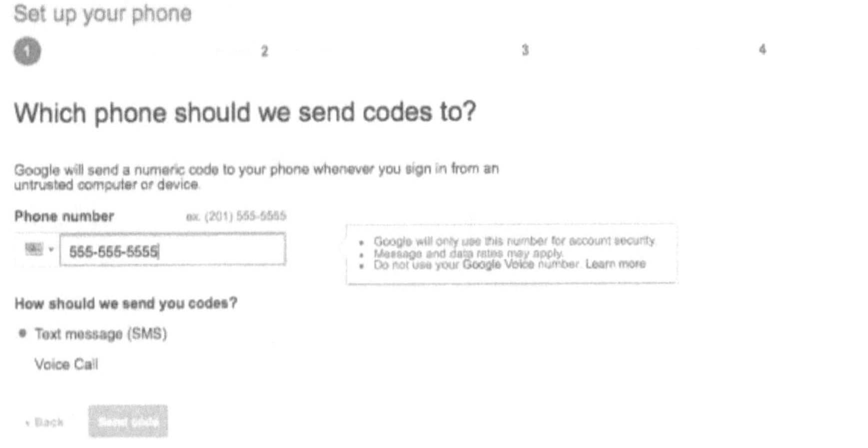

You will receive a code from Google to the mobile number you entered.

Enter the code you received and click verify

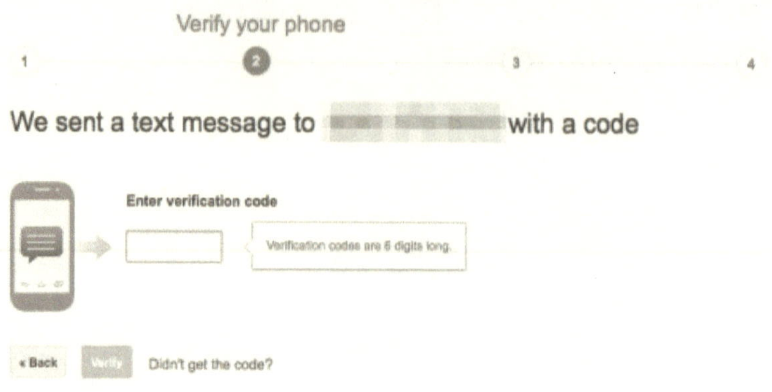

Choose whether or not to add your current computer as a trusted device. If you add your computer as trusted device, you don't have to do verification every time you login.

Anyhow please remember that you have to verify every thirty days

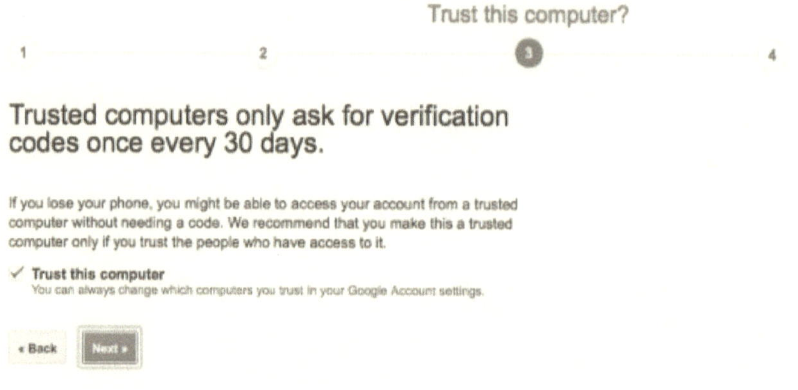

Click the trust this computer checkbox and click next.

Then in the next screen, click confirms and that's it you are now secured. You need your mobile near you to login in, every time you login you will get a code from Google, and you have to enter it when you sign in.

There are many advantages; no one can login to your Gmail account and any Google account without access to your mobile phone. But I am not using this because if I forget my mobile phone at home and go to office , or I lose my mobile phone somewhere , then there is a risk of my Gmail account getting locked so I just don't use this two step verification thing.

Coming back to the sign in and security page, (Change password recovery options)

Below the two step verification toggle, there is your present recovery email and recovery phone. You can click it to change. You will have to sign in again and then edit the email and click done.

It is the same for phone number too.

Scroll down a little and you will see Device activity & notifications. In that heading you can see recent security events, recently used devices.

Then security alert settings, click manage settings to see them.

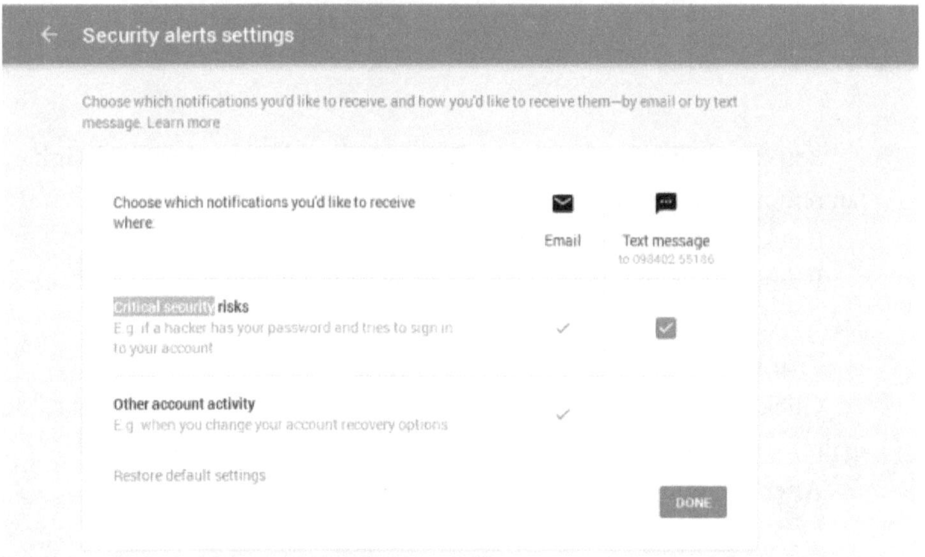

Choose whether you want security alerts in your email or mobile phone (as sms) or in both.

Then click done.

If you think the default settings are better, click Restore default settings link

Then click done

Then click the white arrow on the top left to go back and scroll down.

You will see connected apps and sites,

You can click manage apps link to see what all apps you use

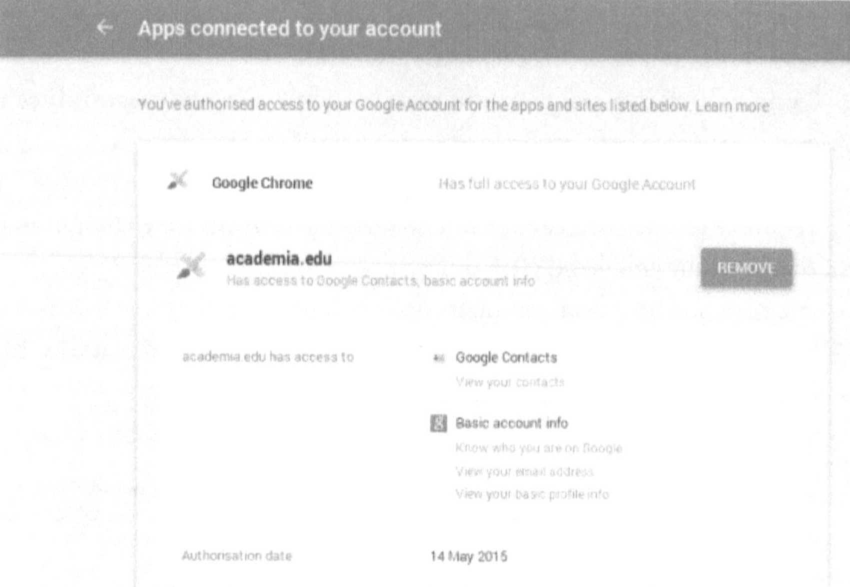

You can click on each apps name to see what all rights and access it has, you can remove that app by clicking the remove button in the right

Click the white arrow to go back

Below the Apps connected to your account panel, you will see saved passwords

That shows saved passwords from your chrome and android.

Click manage passwords link and a new tab will open asking you to sign in again.

After you sign in, saved passwords tab will open

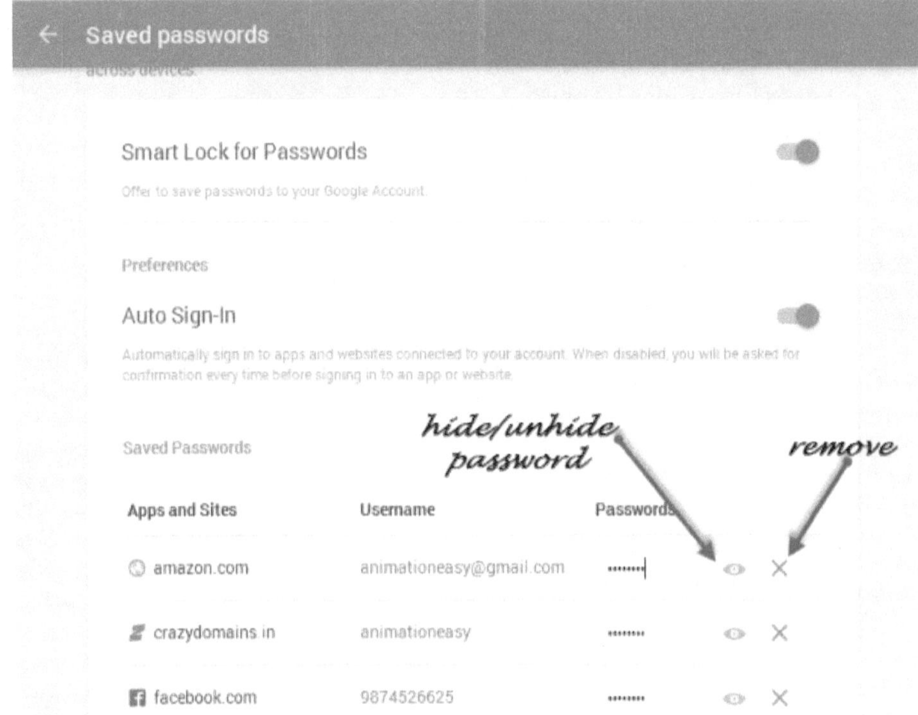

By default, smart lock for passwords is on, auto sign in is on, you can switch them off or on by clicking the blue toggle switches

If you don't like auto sign in you can turn it off, I like auto sign because I sign in to Gmail online in my devices and not in public environments.

Clicking the eye icon you can see your saved passwords, you can click the X icon to remove that particular saved password.

That's all with the security and sign in settings

Other Google account settings: clicking this link opens a new tab showing you My account.

There are sign in and security settings, personal info and privacy, account preferences,

We have finished sign in and security just now. We will see personal info and privacy.

Personal info and privacy has five options

Your personal info

Activity controls

Ads settings

Account overview

Control your content

Let us discuss one by one

Your personal info

By clicking your personal info link, you can edit your name, phone number, about me, birthday etc (all the details you gave when you signed up for Google, except password can be changed here.

Activity controls

Your searches and browsing activity

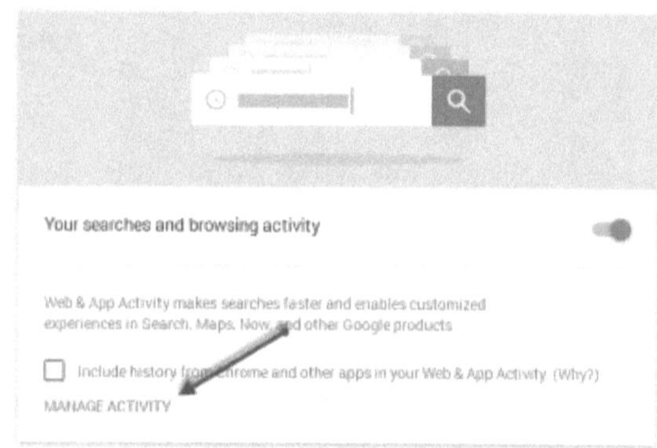

You can see all your past searches which you have done signing in. Click the manage activity link.

Note: you can only view the searches which you have not cleared or deleted from your Google search history.

Places you go

This is switched off by default, you can use the on or off toggle to turn it on

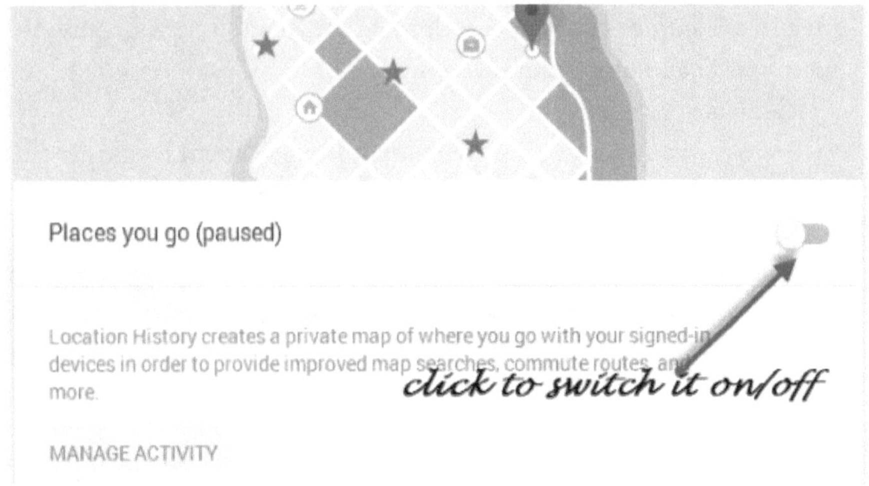

By clicking manage activity link, you can see a Google map showing all the locations you have logged in to Google from

Information from your devices

Device Information stores your contacts, calendars, apps, and other device data to improve your experience across Google. It is switched off by default; you can switch it on using the toggle.

If you turn on, you will get a confirmation screen pop up, click turn on

Click manage activity to view the information

Your voice searches and commands

Voice & Audio Activity helps recognize your voice and improve speech recognition by storing your voice and audio inputs to your account

It is turned off by default, use the toggle button and

Videos you search for on YouTube

It's on by default, click manage activities and you can see your video search history.

You can click the checkbox in the left and then you can delete any particular search. (Just like for your Google search history)

Below the YouTube search history there is ad settings, we have already discussed the ad settings before. Please refer here

Account overview

It is a link to your Google dashboard, click view dashboard; a new screen will open asking you to login. Enter your password and click sign in and wait a few seconds. You will see all your Google products and services accounts in one place. I am not going to give detailed explanation here, because this book doesn't cover anything other than Gmail

Control your content

Here you can take a backup of content from all your Google products.

To download all your data. Click create archive link

Select all the content you want to archive.

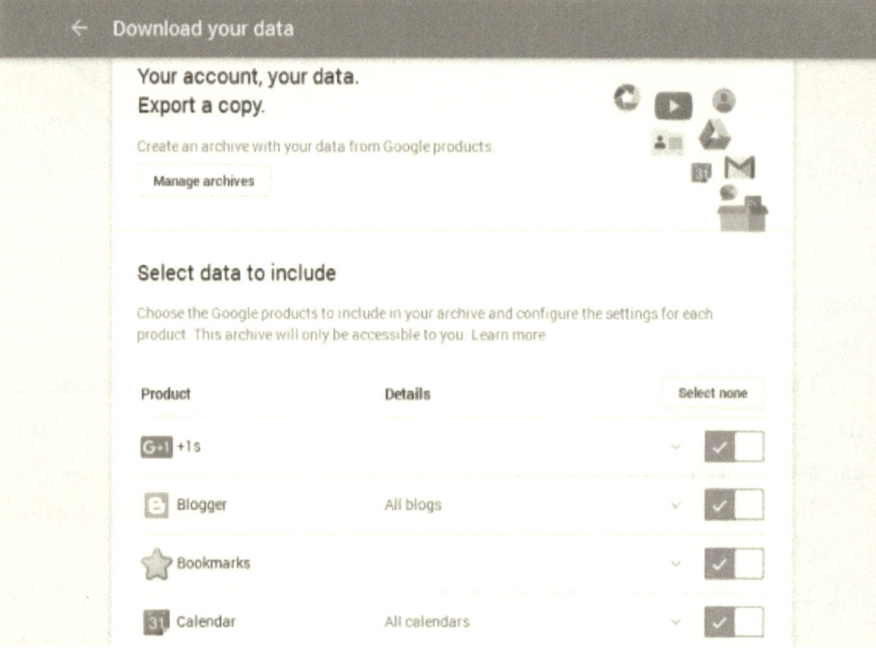

Here all that is you select will show green tick mark as above, clicking that tick mark again will deselect that particular product.

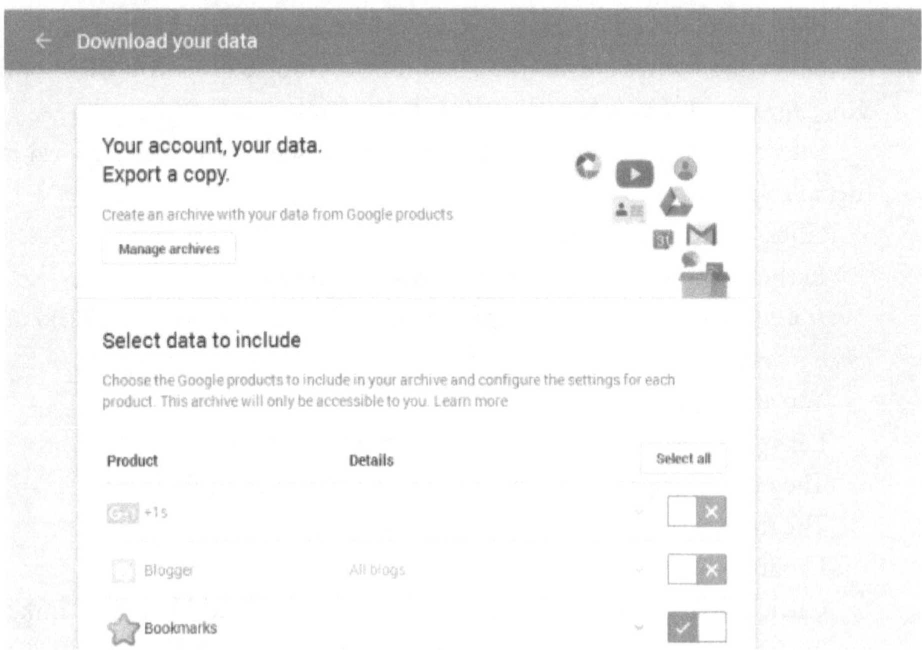

The ones that are not selected shows in grey and has an x mark. You can click it to select it.

Scroll down and select al that you want to and then click next.

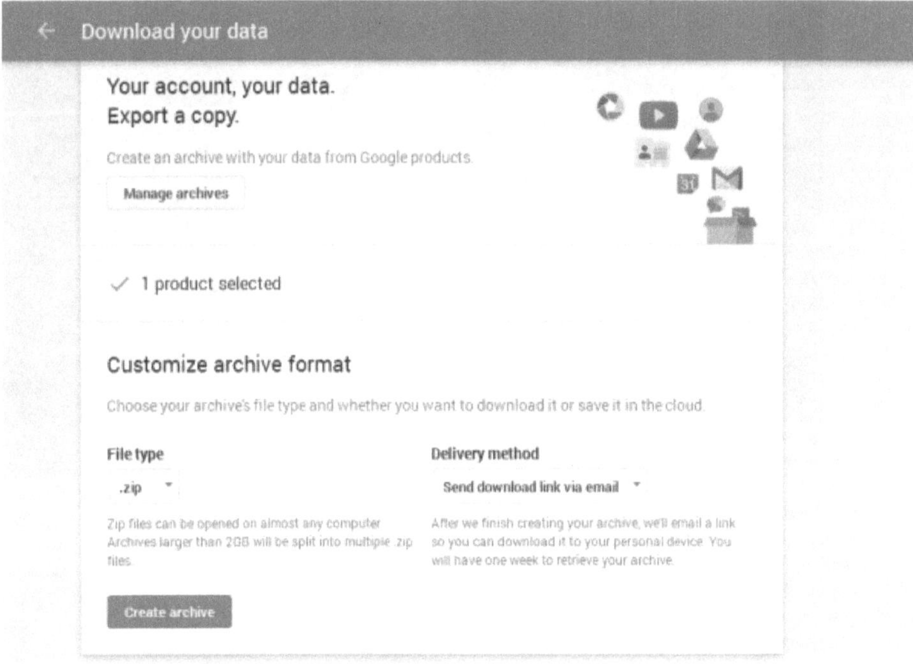

Now it will show how many products have been selected for archive.

Select the file type from the combo box. Google gives you three options .zip. , .tgz, .tbz, I have selected .zip for this example

Select the delivery method, I have selected send download link via email (default option)

Click create archive button.

In the next screen you will see the below message.

It may take some time to complete your archive. Don't worry; we'll email you when it's ready.

You are done.

Let's go back to other Google account settings now.

The next settings we will discuss is Account preferences

The first set of options in account preferences is

Language & Input Tools

Click language and in the next screen you can see add language link. You can use it to add all the languages you speak and understand.

A box pops up where you can search for the languages you know and add by clicking the name of the language which you want to add.

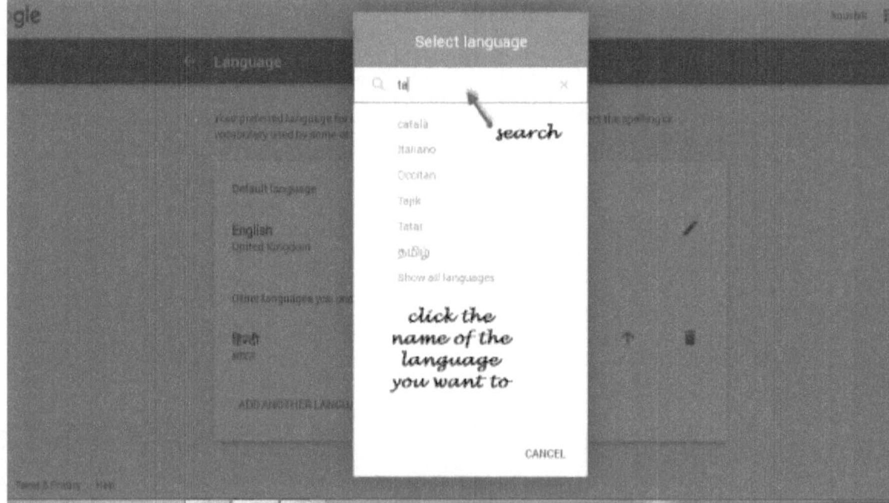

Select the language variant and click okay.

Click the white back arrow to go back

Click input tools

Click select languages and select all the languages you want to use.

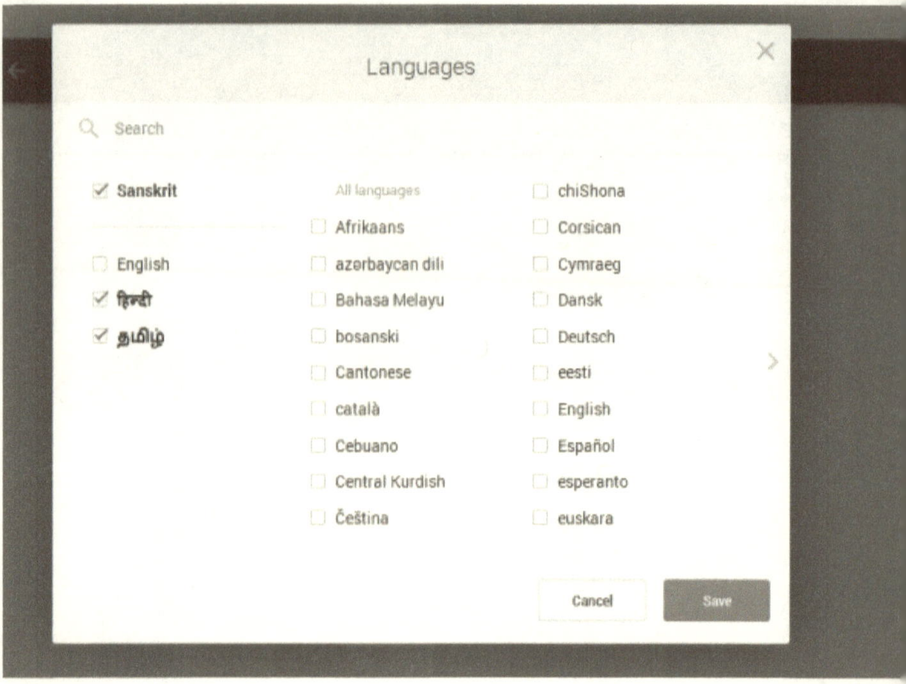

Slick save

In your input tools screen, you can see there are various keyboard options given for each language. You can choose the options which suits you the best and click done.

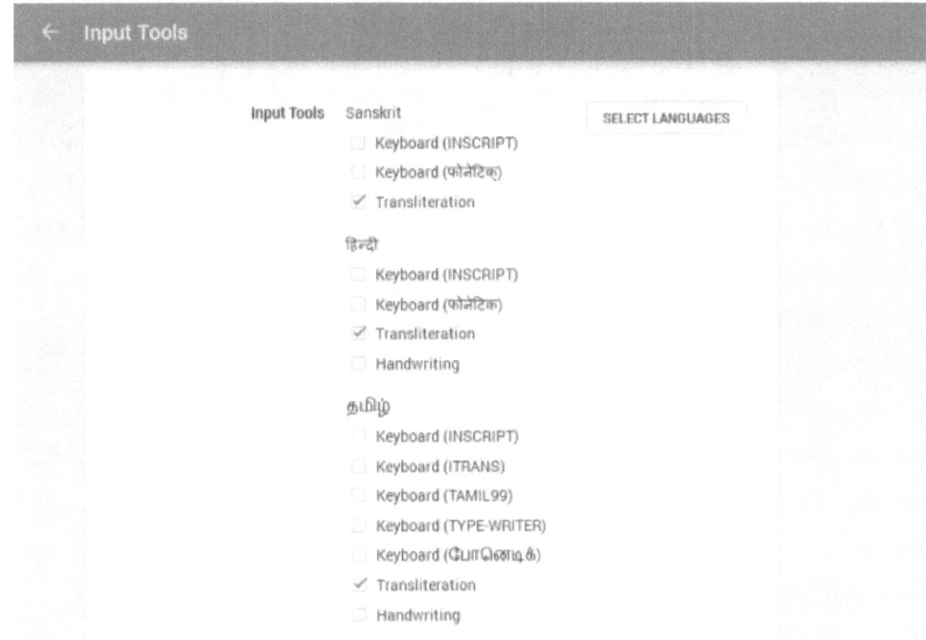

Click the white back arrow and go back

After selecting your input tools you can see in your Gmail, all the languages you can use in a drop down near your gear icon (see image below)

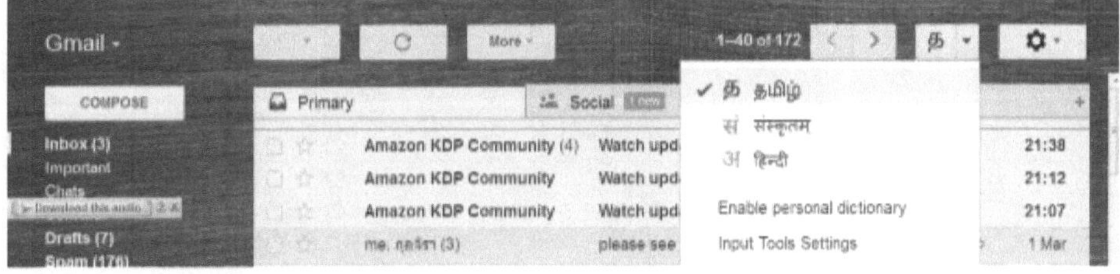

Below Language & Input Tools there is **accessibility.**

You can turn on / off the screen reader from there.

Click the screen reader off/on then select on or off radio button and then click done.

Below that there is Google drive storage, which shows how much space is free and how much is used.

Scroll down a little and you can see

Delete your account or services

You can delete particular Google service for your account by clicking delete product link.

You will be asked to login again. Once you login. You will see a list of Google services you use with a dustbin icon in the right side.

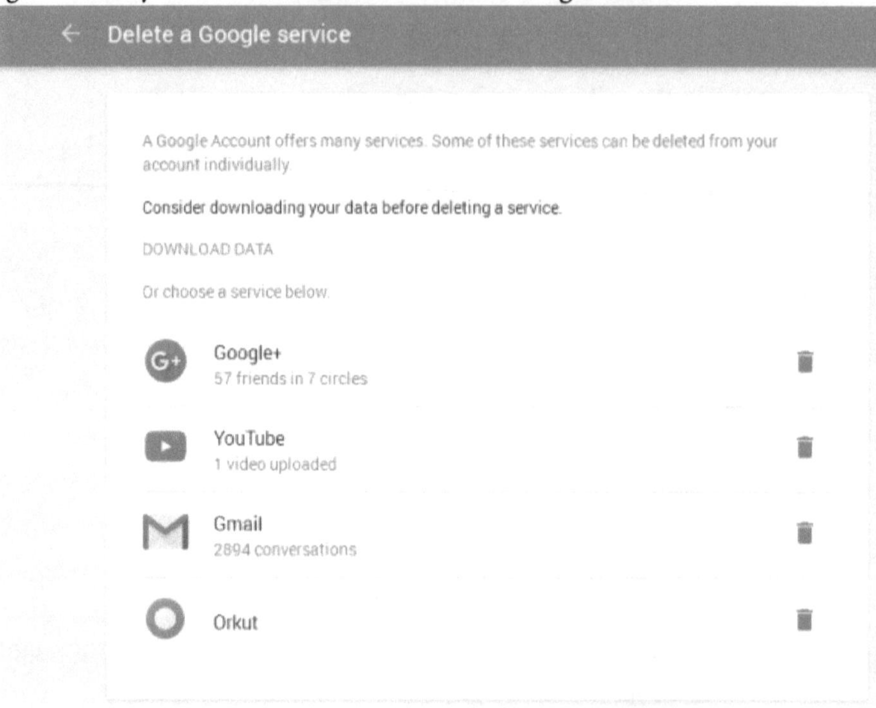

Click the corresponding dust bin icon. Then you will be asked to login again.

For this example I am deleting Orkut

Click yes I want to permanently remove .... checkbox

Click remove orkut button

That particular Google service will permanently be deleted and cannot be retrieved.

Note: Always download your data before deleting a service. You already know by now how to download data from Google.

Deleting your Google account

Click the gear icon then click settings. Click accounts and import and then other account settings. Then click Delete your account or services link

Click delete Google account and data

Sign in to Google again

You will see this screen

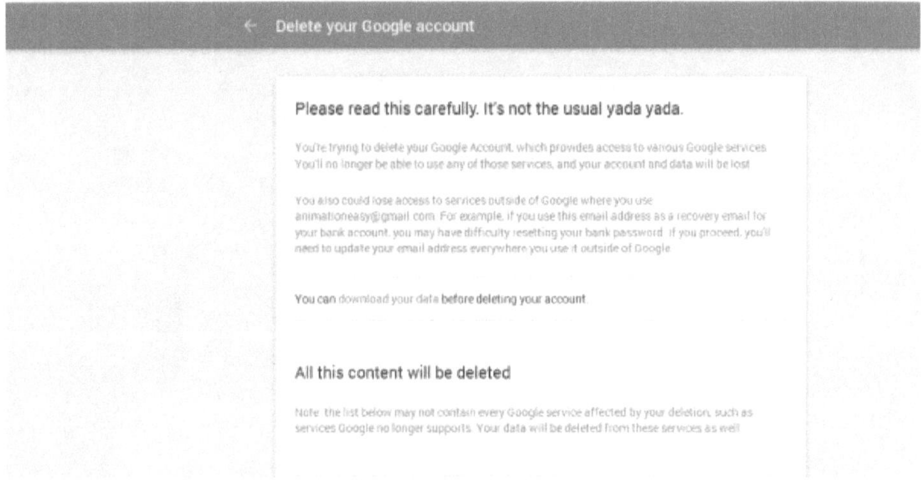

Scroll down and you will see what all will get deleted

Similar to the image shown below.

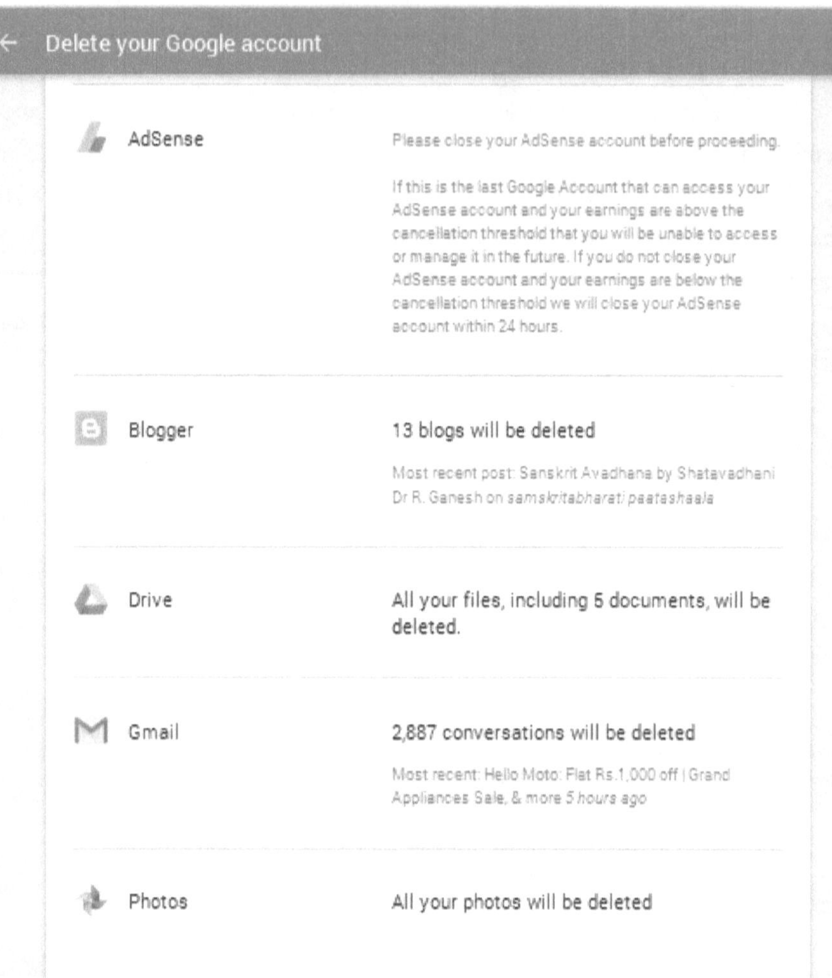

Scroll down

You have to click two check boxes

It says

Yes, I acknowledge that I am still responsible for any charges incurred due to any pending financial transaction and I understand that under certain circumstances my earnings won't be paid out.

Yes, I want to permanently delete this Google account and all its data.

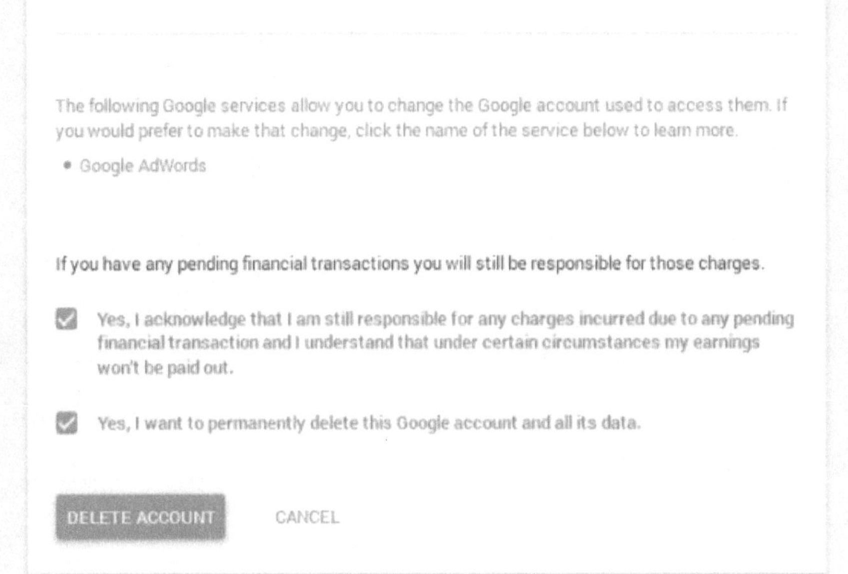

Check those check boxes and it will turn blue (shown in above image)

Click the DELETE ACCOUNT button

And your Google account is deleted and no data can be retrieved any future emails sent to you will not be received by you. I know you know the risk. Only delete your account if you really need to.

Finally we have covered all the options of Other Google Account settings page

The next thing in accounts and import tab of the settings page is

Import Mails and Contacts

Using this option, import from Yahoo!, Hotmail, AOL, or other webmail or POP3 accounts.

Click import mail and contacts link.

A new popup will open,

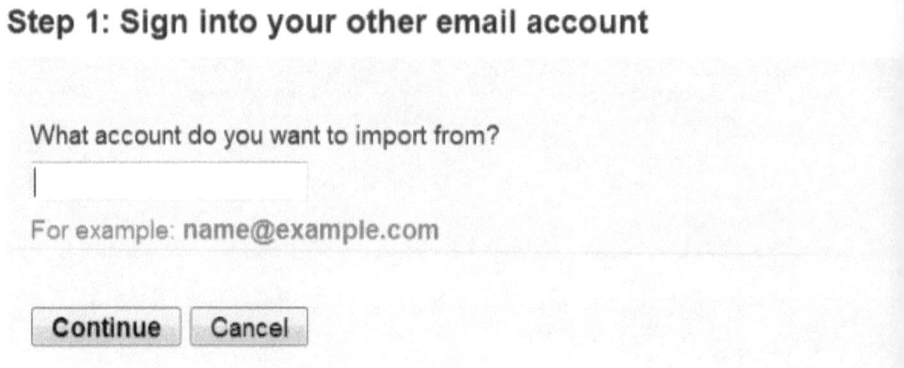

Step 1: Sign into your other email account
What account do you want to import from?
For example: name@example.com
Continue
Cancel

Enter the email address of any account you want to import email and contacts from and click continue

Gmail - Mozilla Firefox
Step 1: Sign into your other email account
What account do you want to import from?
nationeasy@yahoo.com
For example: name@example.com
Checking...
Cancel

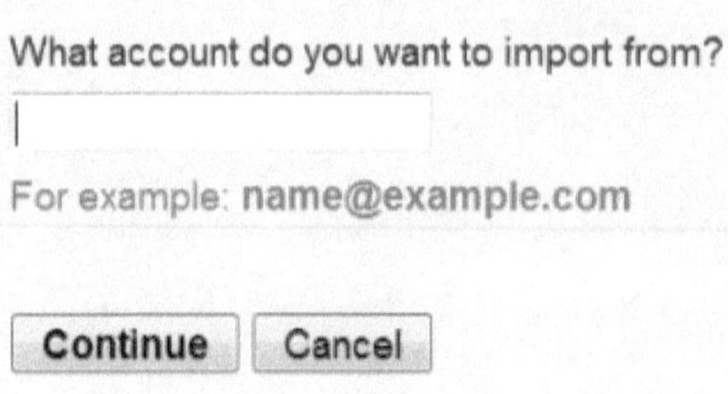

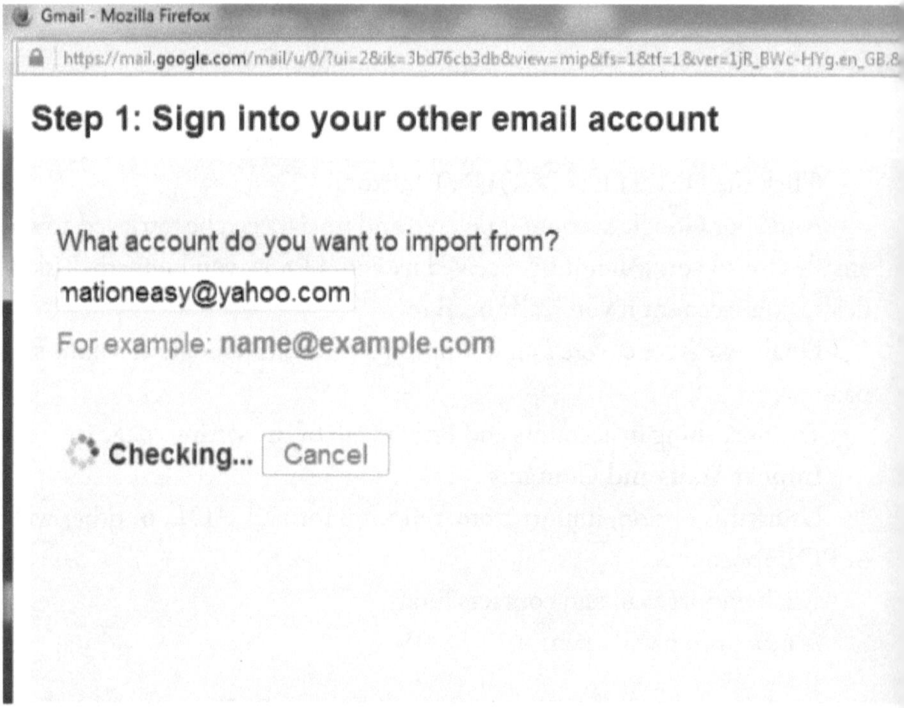

Then you will see the above window popup.

Step 1: Sign into your other email account

Sign in to your other email account to confirm import of emails and/or contacts. Press **Continue** and follow the instructions in the pop-up window.

Importing is powered by ShuttleCloud. By clicking "Continue", you agree to ShuttleCloud's **Terms of Use** and **Privacy Policy**. During import, the connection to the service provider for animationeasy@yahoo.com may be unencrypted.

Continue   Cancel

Click continue, you will be asked to sign in to the account from which you want to import contacts

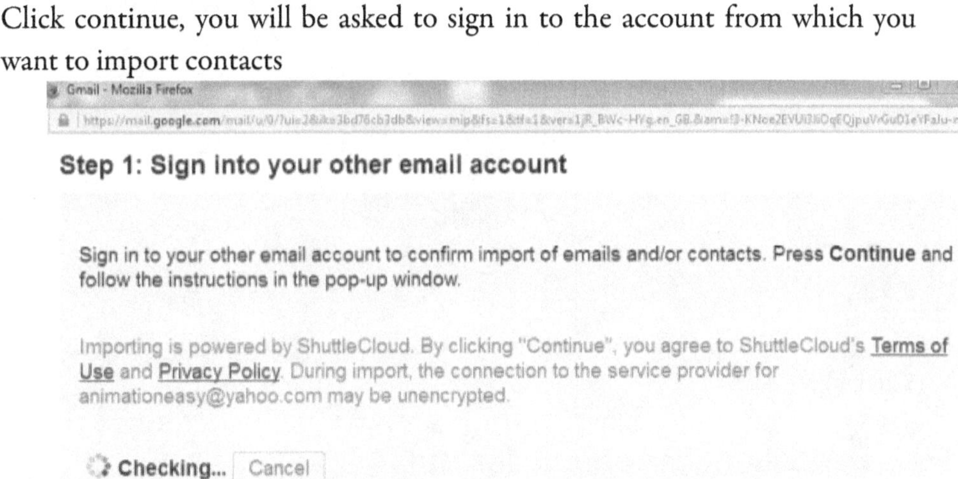

Then you will see the above screen

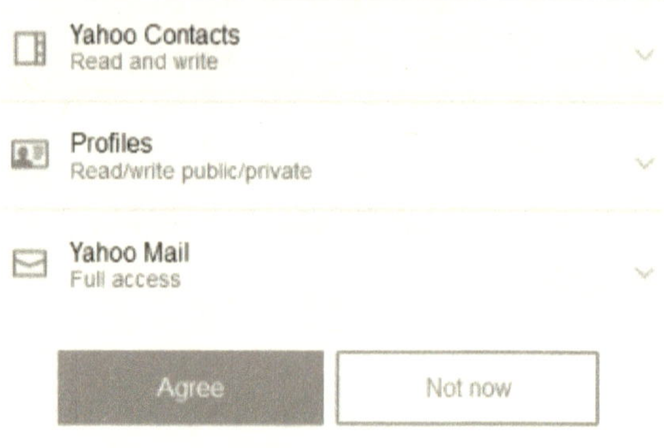

Click agree

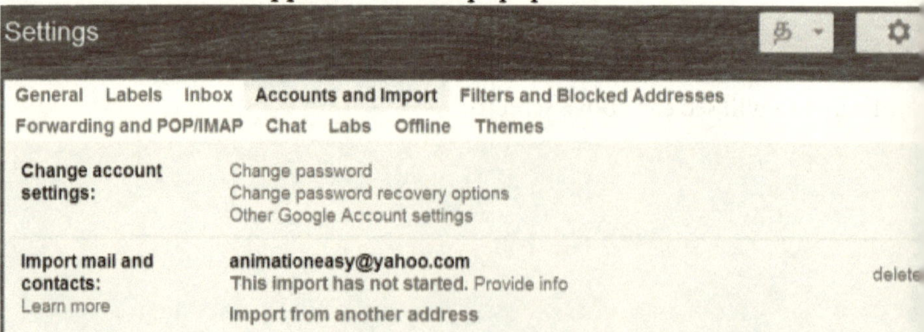

The above screen will appear, close this popup window.

Go back to Gmail account's settings page and click accounts and import you will see "The import has started" in red colour.

You have to wait for some time, I waited three hours, and then I signed in back to Gmail

A popup window appeared (shown below)

Step 2: Import options

Click start import, and your import will start.

For this example, I am selected imports of contacts only

The next window pops up

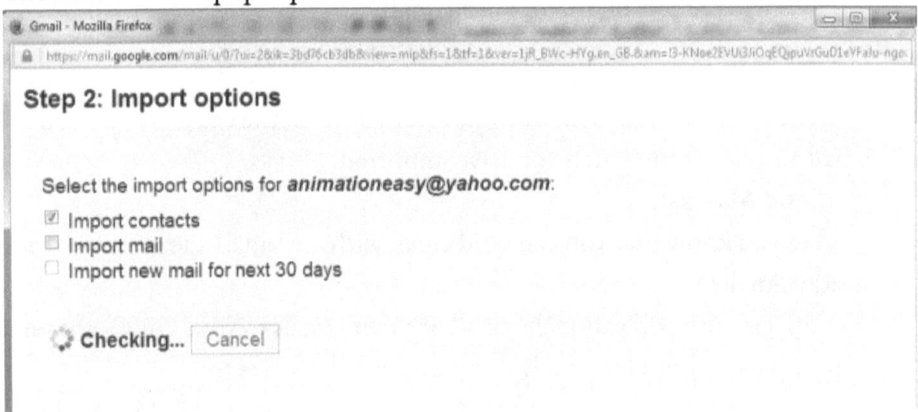

And finally the last pop up appears, click OK

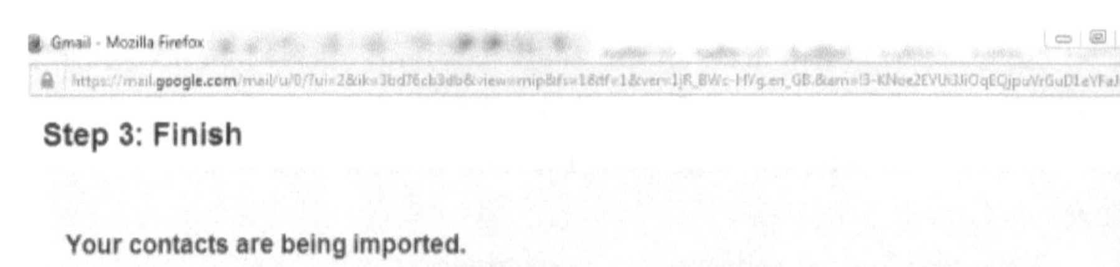

Step 3: Finish

Your contacts are being imported.

It may take several hours (sometimes up to 2 days) before you start to see imported messages.

You can close this window and keep using Gmail or even log out and close your browser – we'll continue importing your mail and/or contacts in the background. To check the status of your import, look under Settings > Accounts and Import.

OK

Now go to settings – accounts and import you will see this imported successfully message

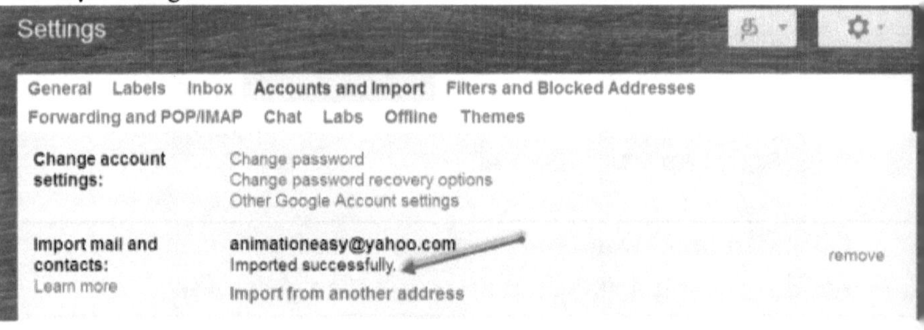

You will see this on top of your Gmail

Import complete! Dismiss
Your contacts from animationeasy@yahoo.com have finished importing.

You can go to your Gmail contacts and find all the contacts you had in that email account from which you have imported.

Send Mail as:

Do you know that you can send email with any email address you own from inside Gmail?

You can also add yahoo, hotmail or other emails to your Gmail account and send emails and receive emails using that email address too.

Just now I have imported contacts from my yahoo email. I have added that email

To add an email address

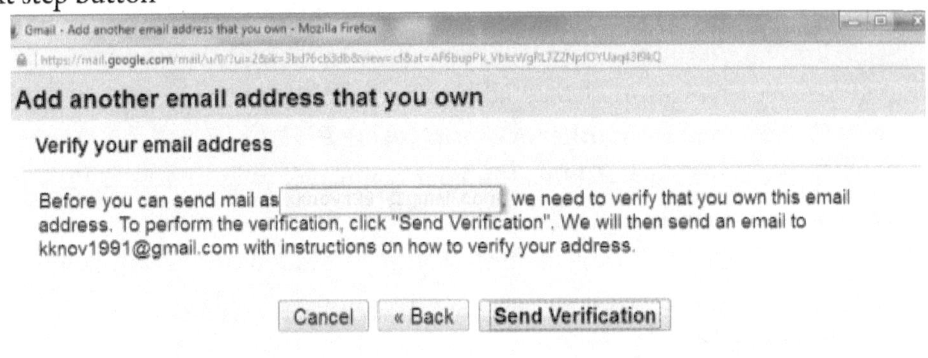

Click add another email address that you own link

Enter name and email address, click the treat as an alias check box and click next step button

You are asked to sign in to that email address which you want to add to Gmail and open the confirmation email sent by Gmail and click the confirmation link.

In this example I signed in to yahoo mail and clicked the confirm link.

Add another email address that you own

Confirm verification and add your email address

An email with a confirmation code was sent to [ ] [Resend email]
To add your email address, do one of the following:

Click the link in the confirmation email   OR   Enter and verify the confirmation code
Verify

Close window

After confirming by clicking that link, from that email account, you will see the above pop up. Click close window link.

You can send email as that email address also.

There are two options you can see below the send email as heading

Reply from the same address to which the message was sent

Always reply from default address

In most times Reply from the same address to which the message was sent will be useful as the receiver will know from whom he is receiving emails. In my opinion this is the best option to choose because there won't be any confusion.

If you want to reply to every email from your default email address, you can click Always reply from default address radio button.

Check email from other accounts (using POP3):

If you maintain a web mail in your company's website, let's say I work in geemyitsolutions.in

My official email id is designer@geemyitsolutions.in. , I will be given an email, password etc. And will be using a login page inside geemyitsolutions.in to check emails.

But I don't want to do that, I want those emails to be forwarded to my Gmail so I can check and respond to messages from official email id from inside Gmail.

I can use this feature.

To add a POP3 account, click the Add a POP3 mail account that you own link

A window pops up.

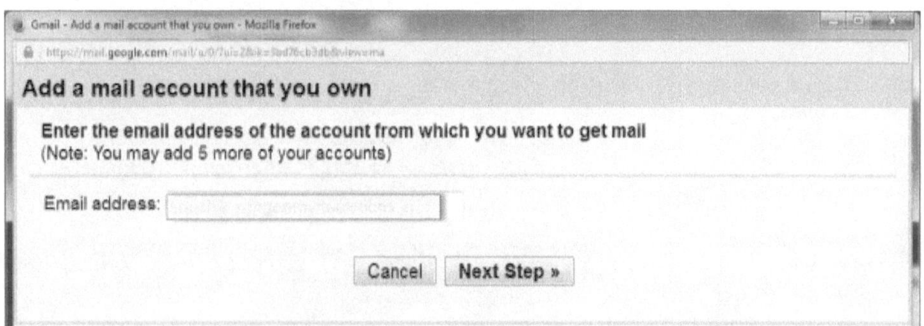

Enter your web email id. name@example.com and click next step button.

Enter the username and password of your pop3 account

Get the port information and pop server information from your company and add that.

You can click leave a copy of retrieved message on the server.

Always use a secure connection (SSL) when retrieving mail checkbox

It's better to have a backup.

Click the Add account button.

Grant access to your account: This comes in very handy if you are working in a company and your official email is to be shared by a number of employees or if you are one of the partners in the business and you want all your partners to have access to the official email of the firm. I know you can do this by sharing the password of that email account. That is no so secure. It may pave way to unwanted circumstances so Gmail provides you with a professional way to share an email account among the partners.

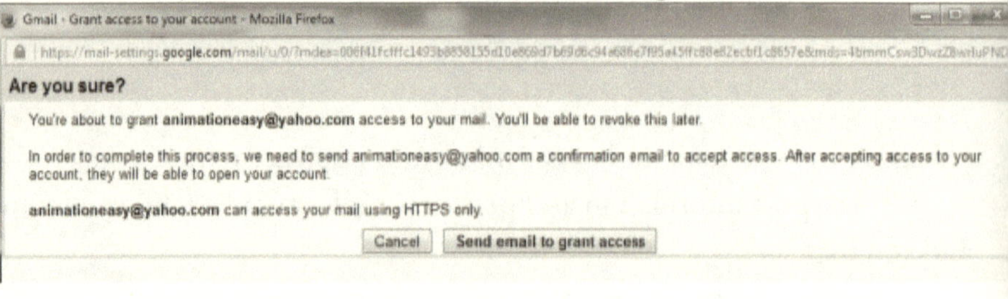

Grant access to your account:
(Allow others to read and send mail on your behalf)
Learn more

Add additional storage:

Add another account

○ **Mark conversation as read when opened by others**
○ **Leave conversation as unread when opened by others**

You are currently using 0.89 GB (5%) of your 15 GB.
Need more space? Purchase additional storage

Click add another account link.

Grant access to your account

Specify a Google Account holder to access your account.
This person will be able to sign in to your account to read, delete and send mail on your behalf. They won't be able to change your account settings or your password.

Email address: [   ]

Cancel   **Next Step »**

A new window pops up enter the email address of your partner with whom you want to share your account and click the "Next step button".

Are you sure?

You're about to grant animationeasy@yahoo.com access to your mail. You'll be able to revoke this later.

In order to complete this process, we need to send animationeasy@yahoo.com a confirmation email to accept access. After accepting access to your account, they will be able to open your account.

animationeasy@yahoo.com can access your mail using HTTPS only.

Cancel   **Send email to grant access**

Click the send email to grant access button

Granted

A confirmation request has been sent to **animationeasy@yahoo.com**. Once they accept the request, they'll have access to your mail. You can always revoke this later.

You will see the Granted message.

Your partner should confirm this by clicking a link sent by Gmail within 24 hours.

Then he can login to this email account and have access to your email

Immediately after that email is sent you will see a warning on top of the screen in your Gmail account (shown below)

You can always deny the access by deleting the email address from the Grant access to your account: (use it only when really needed)

You have two options open to you to choose when you grant access to other emails

Mark conversation as read when opened by others radio button and Leave conversation as unread when opened by others radio button, choose the option which is apt to your needs.

Below that you will see storage information

Filters and Blocked addresses tab

We have already discussed about this tab while creating filters please refer here
Forwarding and POP/IMAP

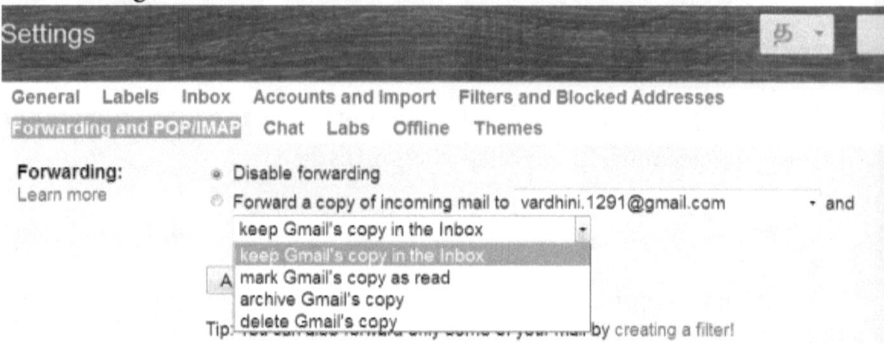

By now you already know about forwarding your emails to another account.

You may have also read how to use filters to forward selective emails to specific addresses

To forward all the emails to another email address, just add that email address as forwarding email address as shown before and click Forward a copy of incoming email to and choose the email address you have added from the combo box and choose keep Gmail's copy in the inbox or any other option.

POP Download:

If you want to use Gmail offline, using any software like Microsoft outlook, Eudora or Netscape mail you can do that.

Click Enable POP for mail that arrives from now on radio button.

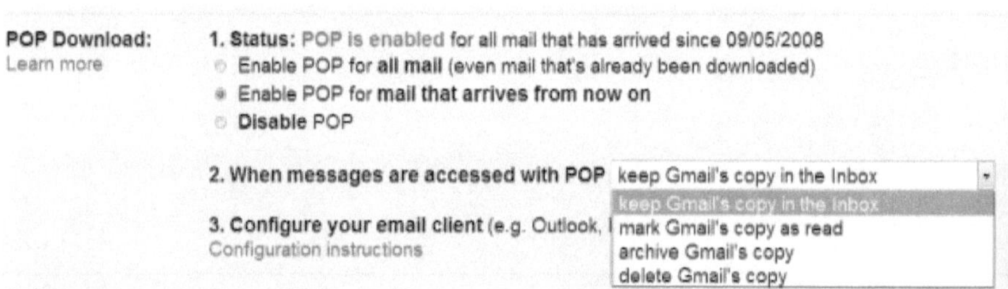

Then from when messages are accessed with pop combo box choose the option which suits you best.

I always select Archive Gmail's copy so you won't get confusion

Click saves changes button.

In your settings in enable pop section you should see a POP is enabled status message in green colour before you can configure your email client.

POP Download: **1. Status:** POP is enabled for all mail that has arrived since 09/05/2008

If you don't get that message, log in to Gmail after some time you will see that message.

Configuring Outlook

Open Outlook

Click the **Tools** menu, and select **Accounts** or **Account Settings...**

On the **E-mail** tab, click **New...**

If you are prompted to **Choose E-mail Service**, select **POP3**

Now enter these details

POP3 Host: pop.gmail.com

POP3 Port: 995

TLS Protocol: ON

POP3 Username: username@gmail.com

POP3 Password: (your Gmail password)

SMTP Host: smtp.Gmail.com

SMTP Port: 587

SSL Protocol: OFF

TLS Protocol: ON

SMTP Username: (your Gmail username)

SMTP Password: (your Gmail password)

After configuring your outlook with these settings if you still have problems in fetching and sending email from your client

https://accounts.Google.com/DisplayUnlockCaptcha[1]

Click the link above and login to Gmail account and then click continue.

---

1.   https://accounts.google.com/DisplayUnlockCaptcha

I explained you about POP but Gmail recommends the use of IMAP instead of POP

What is the main difference between IMAP and POP and why Gmail recommends IMAP?

Let me tell you one difference and you will be convicted to use IMAP instead of POP

If you use POP your Gmail account will not be updated. For example if you delete an email in your Email client (say outlook for example) your Gmail server (online Gmail account) will still contain the email which you deleted using your email client.

Are you convinced now? If yes

Click enable IMAP radio button.

IMAP Access:
(access Gmail from other clients using IMAP)
Learn more

Status: IMAP is disabled
- Enable IMAP
- Disable IMAP

When I mark a message in IMAP as deleted:
- Auto-Expunge on - Immediately update the server. (default)
- Auto-Expunge off - Wait for the client to update the server.

When a message is marked as deleted and expunged from the last visible IMAP folder:
- Archive the message (default)
- Move the message to the Bin
- Immediately delete the message forever

Click Auto-Expunge on - Immediately update the server. (default) radio button (it's already selected by default , leave it as it is)

It is the settings which deletes the emails in your Gmail server when you delete them in your email client.

Folder Size Limits

Click do not limit the number of messages in an IMAP folder (default) radio button

Click disable POP

Click save changes

Now you have to configure your favourite email client.

Use the table below to update your client with the correct information.

Incoming Mail (IMAP) Server:	imap.Gmail.com **Requires SSL**: Yes **Port**: 993
Outgoing Mail (SMTP) Server:	smtp.Gmail.com **Use Authentication**: Yes **Port for SSL:**: 465 or 587 Use same settings as incoming mail server
Full Name or Display Name:	[your name]
Account Name or User Name:	your full email address (including @Gmail.com or @your_domain.com)
Email Address:	your full email address (including @Gmail.com or @your_domain.com)
Password:	your Gmail password

Chat Tab

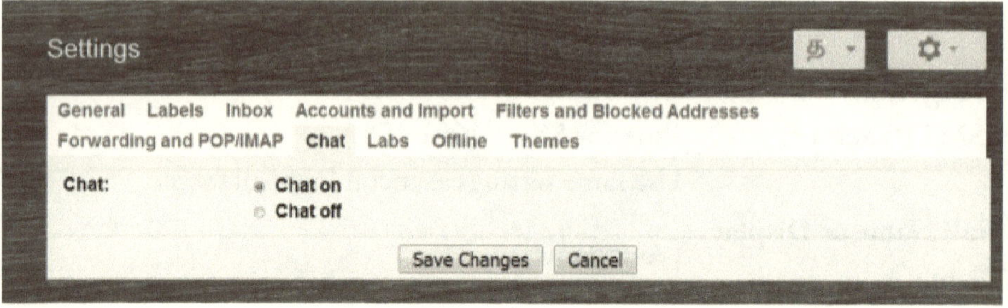

You can enable or disable chat here by click chat on or chat of radio button

Labs Tab

Google labs is where Google checks and releases new features in their products. You can search for a good feature in labs and try to use it, if you don't like it you can also opt out. (disable) that. Some of the successful features tested through Google labs may be implemented by Google permanently in their products. This also means any new feature being tested in Google will be available through labs.

I am not going to explain any of the Lab features here because it changes from time to time.

Try out the features if you get any problem you can contact me.

Offline

Click install Gmail offline link

Note you should click this when you are logged in through your Chrome browser because 'Install Gmail offline' is a chrome plug-in

You would see this page, click add to chrome button

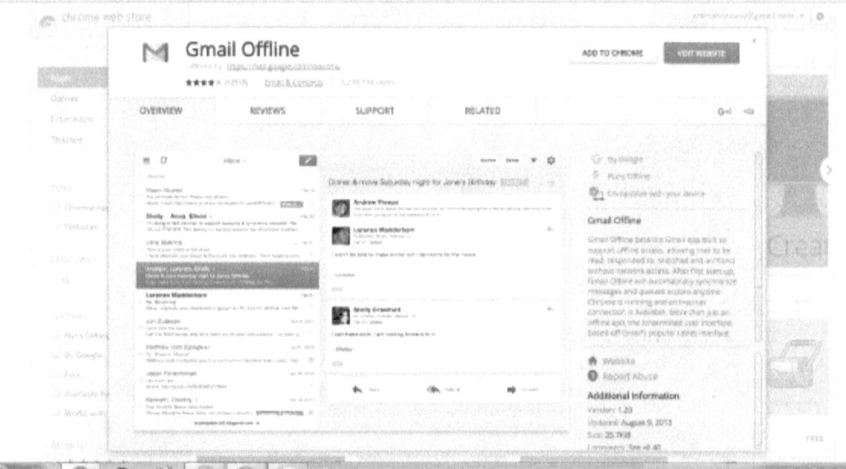

Caution: there are many bad reviews and I am not using Gmail offline, please use it at your own risk.

Click add app

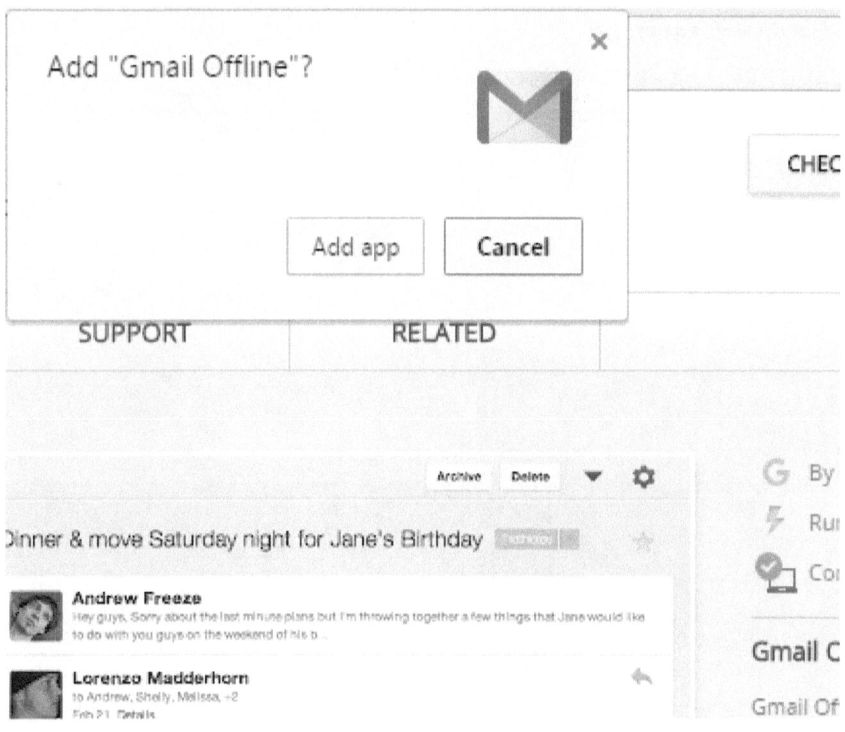
Add "Gmail Offline"?
Add app
Cancel
CHEC
SUPPORT
RELATED
Archive
Delete
Dinner & move Saturday night for Jane's Birthday
Andrew Freeze
Hey guys, Sorry about the last minute plans but I'm throwing together a few things that Jane would like to do with you guys on the weekend of his b...
Lorenzo Madderhorn
to Andrew, Shelly, Melissa, +2
Feb 21 Details
By
Ru
Co
Gmail C
Gmail Of

Keyboard shortcuts

There are nice keyboard shortcuts to speed up your jobs in Gmail
First let me list the keyboard shortcuts which are always available for you.

Shortcut Key	Definition	Action
Ctrl + Enter Mac: ⌘ + **Enter**	Send message	After composing your message, use this combination to send it.
Ctrl + . Mac: ⌘ + **.**	Advance to next window	Use this shortcut to move the cursor to the next chat or compose window, or to the main window.
Ctrl + , Mac: ⌘ + **,**	Go to previous window	Use this shortcut to move the cursor to the previous chat or compose window, or to the main window.
Ctrl + Shift + c Mac: ⌘ + **Shift + c**	Add Cc recipients	While composing, takes you to the Cc field to add new recipients.
Ctrl + Shift + b Mac: ⌘ + **Shift + b**	Add Bcc recipients	While composing, takes you to the Bcc field to add new blind recipients.
Ctrl + Shift + f Mac: ⌘ + **Shift + f**	Change "from" address	While composing, takes you to the From field to change your sending address. This shortcut only works if you have configured additional sending addresses.
Shift + Esc	Focus main window	Use this shortcut to move the cursor to the main window.

There are more shortcuts which you can use in Gmail but first you have to enable keyboard shortcuts in Gmail. Let's see how to do that

Click the ⚙ gear in the top right and select Settings.
Find the "Keyboard shortcuts" section and select Keyboard shortcuts on.
Click Save Changes at the bottom of the page.

98

Shortcut Key	Definition	Action
c	Compose	Allows you to compose a new message. **Shift** + **c** allows you to compose a message in a new window.
d	Compose in a new tab	Opens a compose window in a new tab.
/	Search	Puts your cursor in the search box.
k	Move to newer conversation	Opens or moves your cursor to a more recent conversation. You can hit **Enter** to expand a conversation.
j	Move to older conversation	Opens or moves your cursor to the next oldest conversation. You can hit **Enter** to expand a conversation.
n	Newer message	In 'Conversation view', moves your cursor to the newer message. You can hit **Enter** to expand or collapse a message.
p	Previous message	In 'Conversation view', moves your cursor to the older message. You can hit **Enter** to expand or collapse a message.
`	Go to next inbox section	If you use an inbox style with tabs or sections, you can quickly navigate to the next section.
~	Go to previous inbox section	If you use an inbox style with tabs or sections, you can quickly navigate to the previous section.
o or **Enter**	Open	Opens your conversation. Also expands or collapses a message if you are in 'Conversation View.'
u	Return to conversation list	Refreshes your page and returns you to the inbox, or list of conversations.
e	Archive	Archive your conversation from any view.
m	Mute	Archives the conversation, and all future messages skip

		the Inbox unless sent or cc'd directly to you.
x	Select conversation	Automatically checks and selects a conversation so that you can archive, apply a label, or choose an action from the drop-down menu to apply to that conversation.
s	Star a message or conversation	Adds or removes a star to a message or conversation. Stars allow you to give a message or conversation a special status.
+	Mark as important	Helps Gmail learn what's important to you by marking misclassified messages. (Specific to Priority Inbox)
-	Mark as unimportant	Helps Gmail learn what's not important to you by marking misclassified messages. (Specific to Priority Inbox)
!	Report spam	Marks a message as spam and removes it from your conversation list.
r	Reply	Replies to the message sender. **Shift** + **r** allows you to reply to a message in a new window. (Only applicable in 'Conversation View.')
a	Reply all	Replies to all message recipients. **Shift** + **a** allows you to reply to all message recipients in a new window. (Only applicable in 'Conversation View.')
f	Forward	Forwards a message. **Shift** + **f** allows you to forward a message in a new window. (Only applicable in 'Conversation View.')
Esc	Escape from input field	Removes the cursor from your current input field.
Ctrl + **s** Mac: ⌘ + **s**	Save draft	Saves the current text as a draft when composing a message. Hold the **Ctrl**/⌘ key while pressing **s** and make sure your cursor is in one of the text fields—either the composition pane, or any of the To, CC, BCC, or Subject fields—when using this shortcut.
#	Delete	Moves the conversation to Trash.

l	Label	Opens the Labels menu to label a conversation.
v	Move to	Moves the conversation from the inbox to a different label, Spam or Trash.
Shift + i	Mark as read	Marks your message as 'read' and skip to a newer message.
Shift + u	Mark as unread	Marks your message as 'unread' so you can go back to it later.
[	Removes from current view and previous	Removes the current view's label from your conversation and moves to the older one.
]	Removes from current view and next	Removes the current view's label from your conversation and moves to the newer one.
{	Archive and previous	Archives the current conversation and moves to the older one.
}	Archive and next	Archives the current conversation and moves to the next one.
z	Undo	Undoes your previous action, if possible (works for actions with an 'undo' link).
Shift + n	Update current conversation	Updates your current conversation when there are new messages.
q	Move cursor to chat search	Moves your cursor directly to the chat search box.
y	Remove from Current View*	Automatically removes the message or conversation from your current view. From 'Inbox,' 'y' means **Archive** From 'Starred,' 'y' means **Unstar**

		From 'Trash,' 'y' means **Move to inbox** From any label, 'y' means **Remove the label** * 'y' has no effect if you're in 'Spam,' 'Sent,' or 'All Mail.'
.	Show more actions	Displays the 'More Actions' drop-down menu.
,	Moves cursor to the first button in your Gmail toolbar	Displays the 'More Actions' drop-down menu.
Ctrl + Down arrow Mac: ⌘ **+ Down arrow**	Opens options in Chat	**Ctrl/⌘ + Down arrow** moves from edit field in your chat window to select the 'Video and more' menu Next, press **Tab** to select the emoticon menu Press **Enter** to open the selected menu
k	Move up a contact	Moves your cursor up in your contact list
j	Move down a contact	Moves your cursor down in your contact list
o or **Enter**	Open	Opens the contact with the cursor next to it.
u	Return to contact list view	Refreshes your page and returns you to the contact list.
e	Remove from Current Group	Removes selected contacts from the group currently being displayed.
x	Select contact	Checks and selects a contact so that you can change group membership or choose an action from the drop-down menu to apply to the contact.

Esc	Escape from input field	Removes the cursor from the current input
#	Delete	Deletes a contact permanently
l	Group membership	Opens the groups button to group contacts
z	Undo	Reverses your previous action, if possible (works for actions with an 'undo' link)

Combo-keys

Use the following combinations of keys to navigate through Gmail.

Shortcut Key	Definition	Action
Tab then **Enter**	Send message	After composing your message, use this combination to send it.
y then **o**	Archive and next	Archives your conversation and moves to the next one.
g then **a**	Go to 'All Mail'	Takes you to 'All Mail,' the storage site for all mail you've ever sent or received (and have not deleted).
g then **s**	Go to 'Starred'	Takes you to all conversations you have starred.
g then **c**	Go to 'Contacts'	Takes you to your Contacts list.
g then **d**	Go to 'Drafts'	Takes you to all drafts you have saved.
g then **l**	Go to 'Label'	Takes you to the search box with the "label:" operator filled in for you.
g then **i**	Go to 'Inbox'	Returns you to the inbox.
g then **t**	Go to 'Sent Mail'	Takes you to all mail you've sent.
* then **a**	Select all	Selects all mail.
* then **n**	Select none	Deselects all mail.
* then **r**	Select read	Selects all mail you've read.
* then **u**	Select unread	Selects all unread mail.
* then **s**	Select starred	Selects all starred mail.
* then **t**	Select unstarred	Selects all unstarred mail.

Search in Gmail

We have discussed already about Gmail's search functionalities while we used filters. Now let us explore some more and learn to use the search feature efficiently to find your emails quickly.

Google help lists the search operators in this page

https://support.Google.com/mail/answer/7190?hl=en[1]

from: - you can either give the email address or the name of the contact

subject: - Subject line.

to: - To line names and addresses.

cc: - Cc field names and addresses.

bcc: - Bcc field names and address in emails you sent.

label: - Mail assigned a label. Replace whitespace characters in label names with hyphens.

is:starred - Starred messages.

is:unread - Unread messages.

is:read - Rad messages.

in: - Messages in a standard view: Drafts, Inbox, Chats, Sent, Spam, Trash and anywhere.

has:attachment - Messages with attachments.

filename: - Search attachment file names and file types.

lang: - Messages in a particular language.

after: - Messages sent after a date (YYYY/MM/DD).

before: - Messages sent before a date (YYYY/MM/DD).

We already know the use of has keyword but I am repeating it here for reference.

has:yellow-star - Messages with a yellow star.

has:red-bang - Messages with a red exclamation mark.

has:yellow-bang - Messages with a yellow exclamation mark.

1.	https://support.google.com/mail/answer/7190?hl=en

has:purple-question - Messages with a purple question mark.

has:orange-guillemet - Messages with two orange forward arrows.

has:blue-info - Messages with a blue i.

has:red-star - Messages with a red star.

has:orange-star - Messages with an orange star.

has:green-star - Messages with a green star.

has:blue-star - Messages with a blue star.

has:purple-star - Messages with a purple star.

Combining Search Terms and Search Operators

"" - Messages containing a phrase (case-insensitive).

OR - Messages containing at least one of two terms or expressions.

- - Messages that do not contain a term or expression.

() - Group search terms or expressions.

By default, Gmail combines search terms and operators with "AND": all criteria must be met.

If you master the use of search in Gmail you can create more complex filters to automate your job with ease.

Using Gmail as an Auto-responder

Sometimes you need to send a template response to many people if you are using Gmail for work. Let's say you are dealing with help and support or something similar from your Gmail. Many times you may need to send the same email to many people. (I am not talking about forwarding the emails to multiple recipients here)

The best solution is to use an auto responder. Many people suggest using of canned messages of Google labs; I think I have found a better solution for you.

With this plug-in you can process the reply of messages in bulk, you can also attach files to your auto responded messages, you can use filters to process emails in combination with this plug-in.

Again this plug-in works in Google chrome only '

https://chrome.Google.com/webstore/detail/email-autoresponder/aohckefanobajaljiobafejcdjjefejl[1]

Go to the above link from Google chrome and click free

Wait for some time

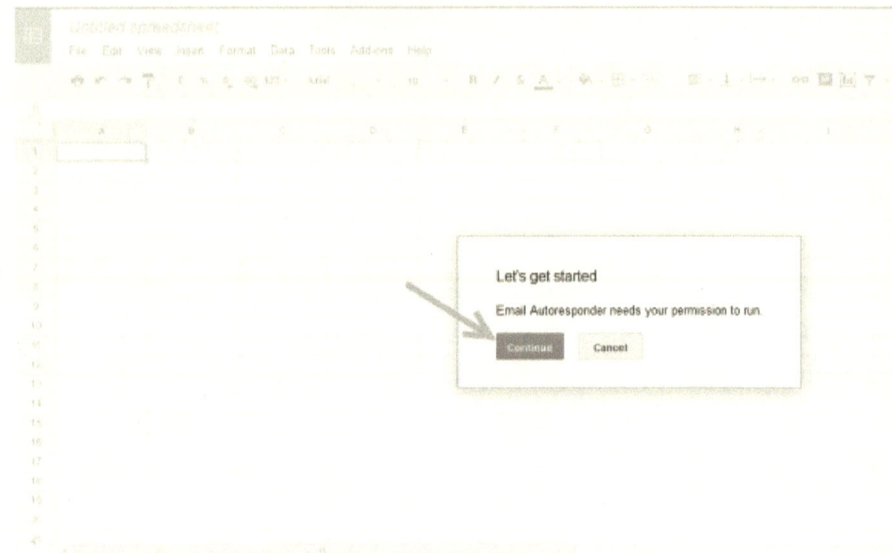

Click continue

After some seconds, click Add-ons, then click Email Autoresponder and click Create New Rule

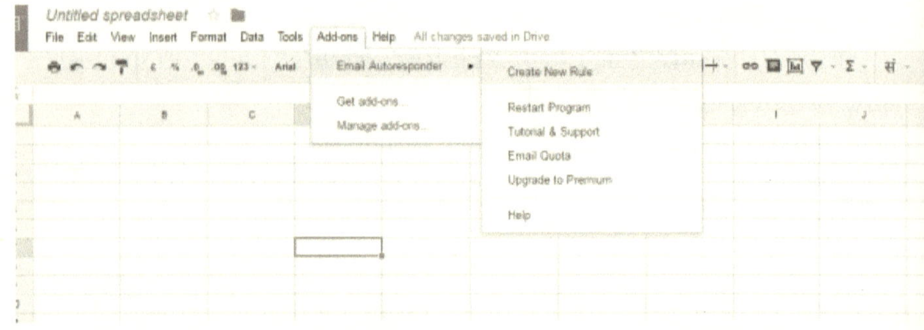

Create New Rule dialog box appears

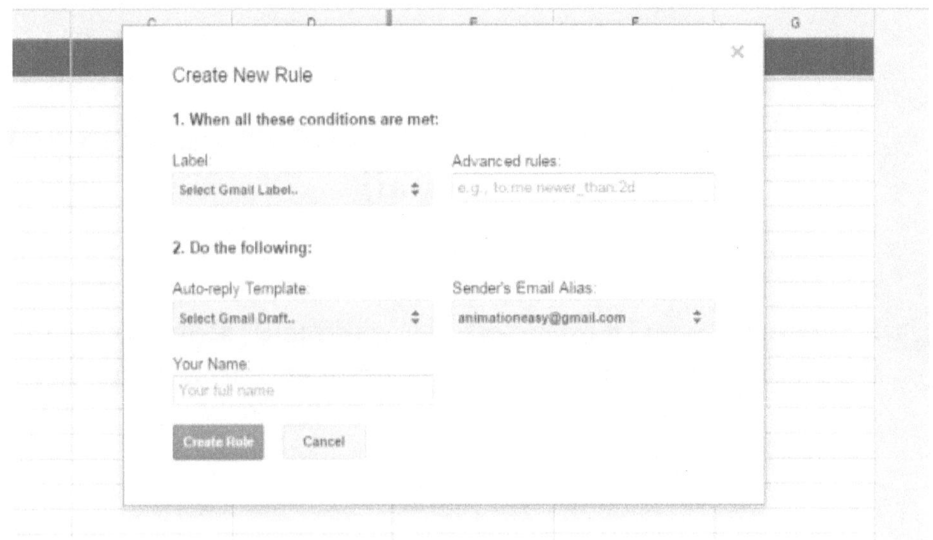

All you will have to do is to write advanced rules and the given text box, apply a label and select an auto reply template (the templates are the drafts you have created in your Gmail account)

If you have not created drafts for auto responds, just go to Gmail and create drafts which you will use in sending replies.

Creating an advance rule is easy it is just using Gmail search operators (just like in filters)

Limitations: free version can only process twenty auto responses per day

Yes I understand that it is a great limitation but definitely better than canned messages because of the limitation that every canned message will be sent from username+*canned.response@Gmail.com*

Sending Scheduled email and reminders with Gmail

If you are using Gmail for your work, you will definitely need to send scheduled emails and reminders. I use a free app which provides me that functionality. The website is lettermelater.

www.lettermelater.com[1]

Click the above link and then click sign up

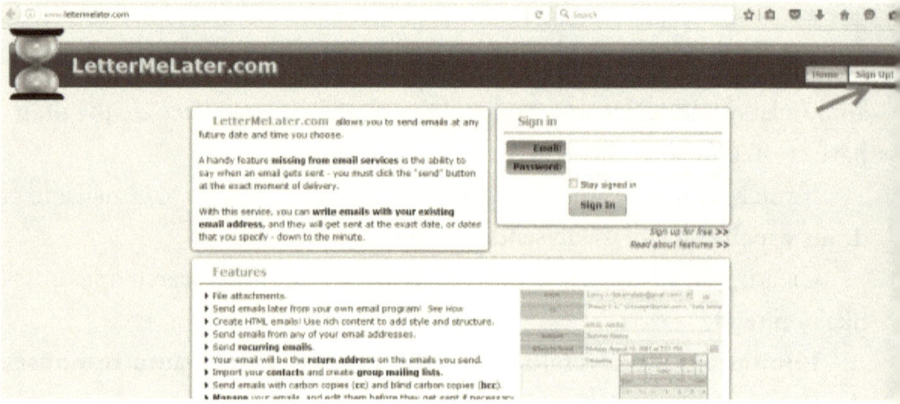

Fill the sign up form and click create account

Login to your Gmail account and click the confirmation link sent by the lettermelater.com

Your account will be activated.

After you click that link you will see the below screen

I am only using the free service offered by this website, there is a paid service offered for **$19.95 USD per year** per email

The limitations of using a free account is

	Free Account	Upgraded Account
➥Number of emails scheduled per month	30	400
➥Number of recipients per email message	3	400
➥Number of recurrences per email message	5	30
➥Size limit of attachments per email message	2MB	10MB
➥Size limit of total attachments per account	10MB	50MB

The services which are offered for free are more than enough for me because mine is a personal account and I use it for work too.

Detailed Profiles of Your Email Contacts

If you want to upgrade the services for business, I consider 19.95 an year is cheap.

Let me show you how to set up a scheduled email with this service.

First let us add contacts there.

Click contact and then click add a new contact

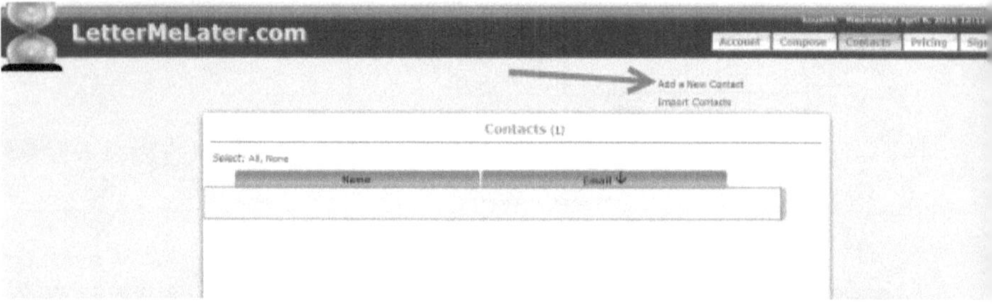

IA new dialogue box appears, enter the name and email you want to add and click add button

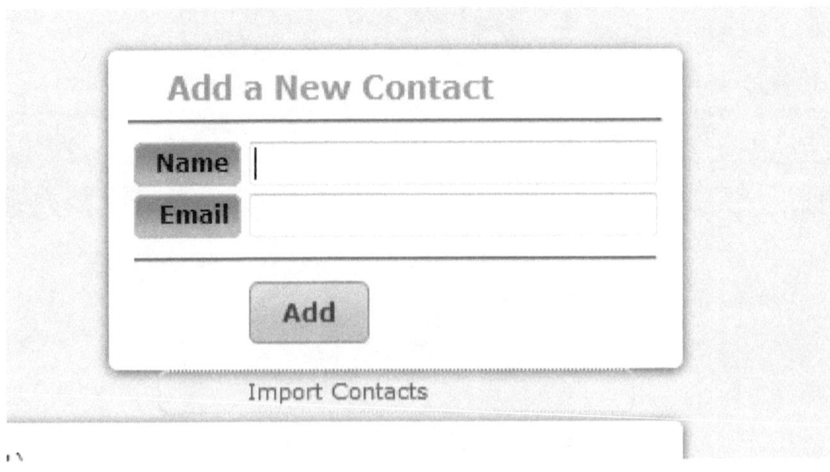

If you want to import contacts from a csv file you can click import contacts
link and then upload a csv file and click import button.

Now that you have finished importing contacts

Click compose and you will see a regular web mail composer interface.

It's just like creating your email draft.

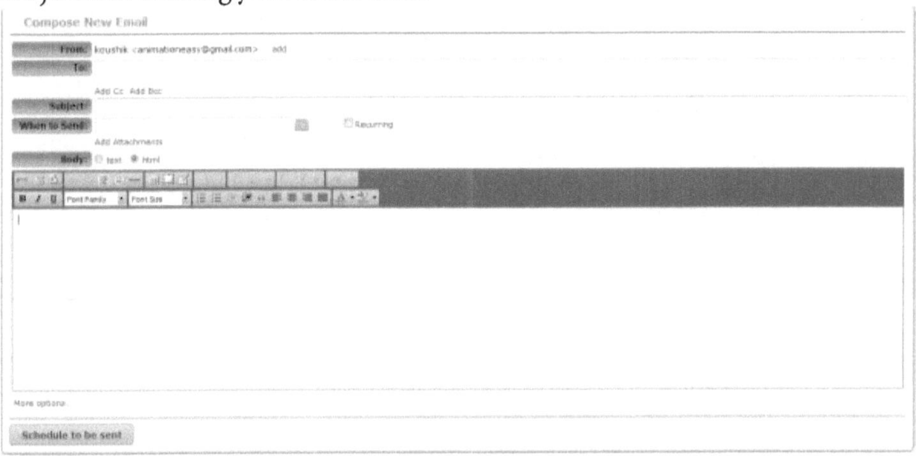

The only thing which is new is when to send header:

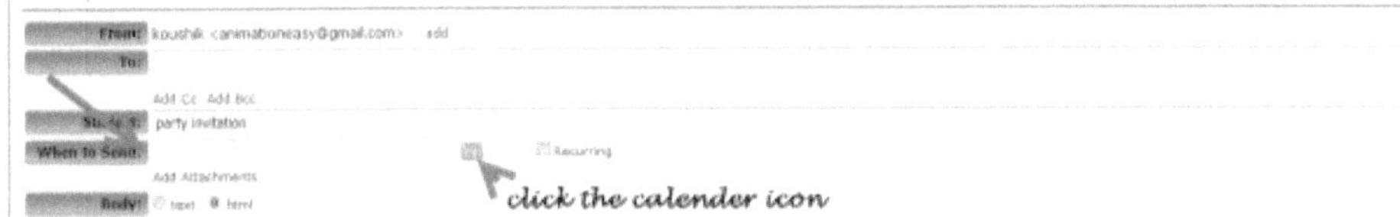

A calendar pops up; select the date when you would like to send this email

You can also send recurring emails in regular intervals by clicking the recurring check box

Then select start date and end date and set interval

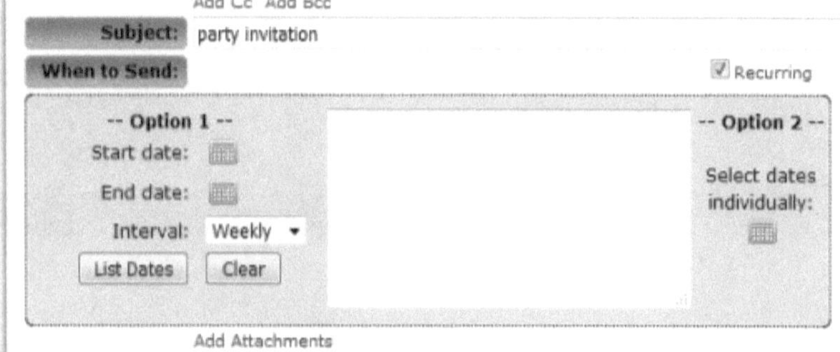

You can set intervals as weekly, monthly or even yearly. Select from the combo box

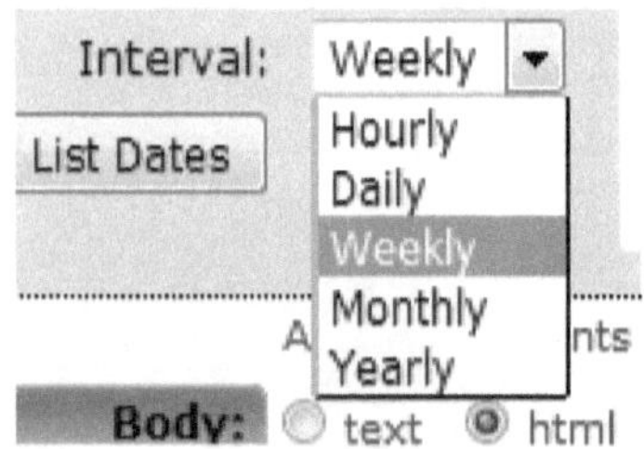

Below the text area there is a link called more options click it

There are two options under the list.

You can click the hide and remind check boxes if you need. See the description in the above image.

After editing your emails and creating the draft completely, click schedule to be sent button.

Detailed profile of your contacts using Full contact

Many of you may have used rapportive but now rapportive has changed a lot due to its takeover by linkedin. I will show you an alternative to it

Full contact

https://chrome.Google.com/webstore/detail/fullcontact-for-Gmail/cnaibnehbbinoohhjafknihmlopdhhip[1]?

Copy and paste the above link in your Google chrome browser's address bar

Then click add to chrome and add the extension

You will be asked to login to your Gmail account

Then you will see this screen inside your Gmail account

---

1.   https://chrome.google.com/webstore/detail/fullcontact-for-gmail/
cnaibnehbbinoohhjafknihmlopdhhip

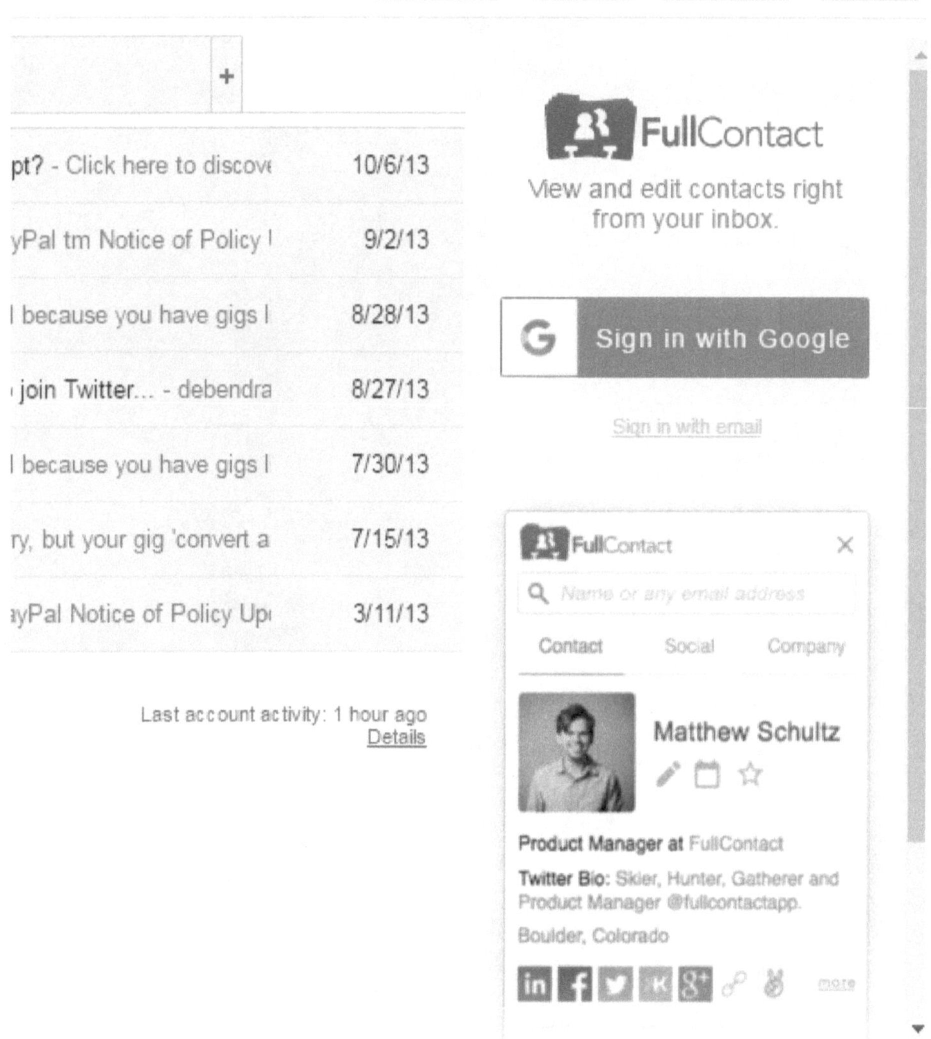

Click sign in with Google and then a new tab will open

Click allow
Then click got it from inside your Gmail (see below screenshot)

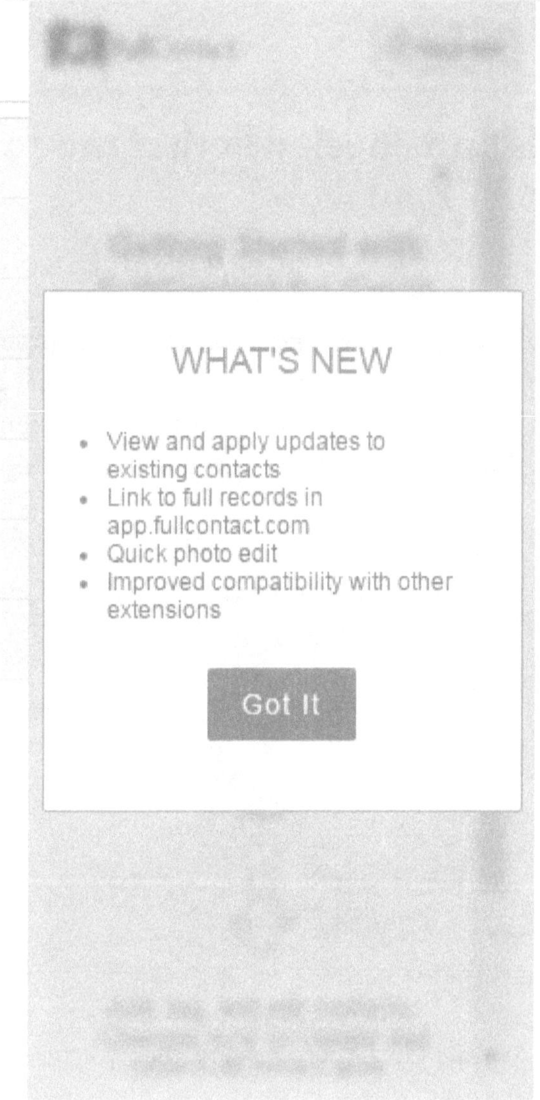

Open an email thread or hover over a contact to see a profile of the person.

Use the search bar to search contacts, email addresses, and tags.

Add, tag, and edit contacts. Changes sync to Google

Now when you open emails you can see detailed profile on the right side

Track your emails and check whether they are read

Whether you are using Gmail for work or even personal; you would probably wish to see whether the people open your emails or not. When you don't get a reply you will most probably be very curious to know whether the person has read your email but not replied you. There is a tool do check that for you.

Streak

https://www.streak.com/email-tracking-in-Gmail[1]

Open the above link from chrome and then click install Streak for Gmail

You will be asked to login to your Gmail account and then a screen pops up

---

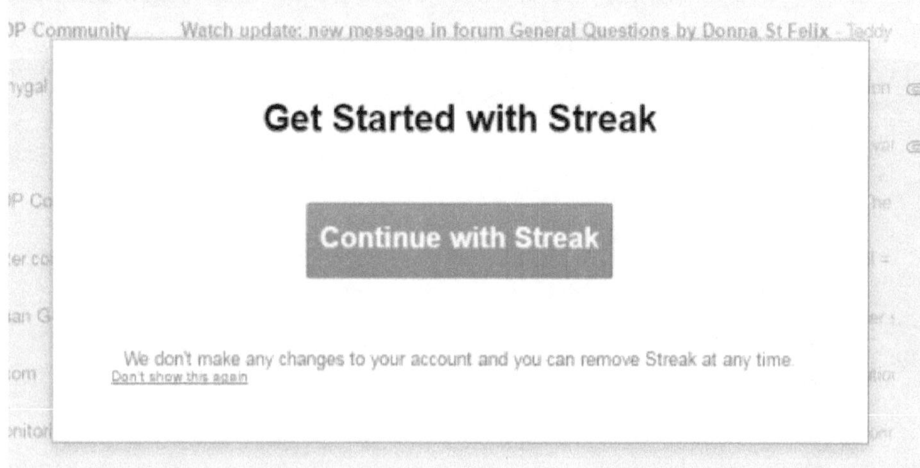

Click continue with streak
Another window pops up.

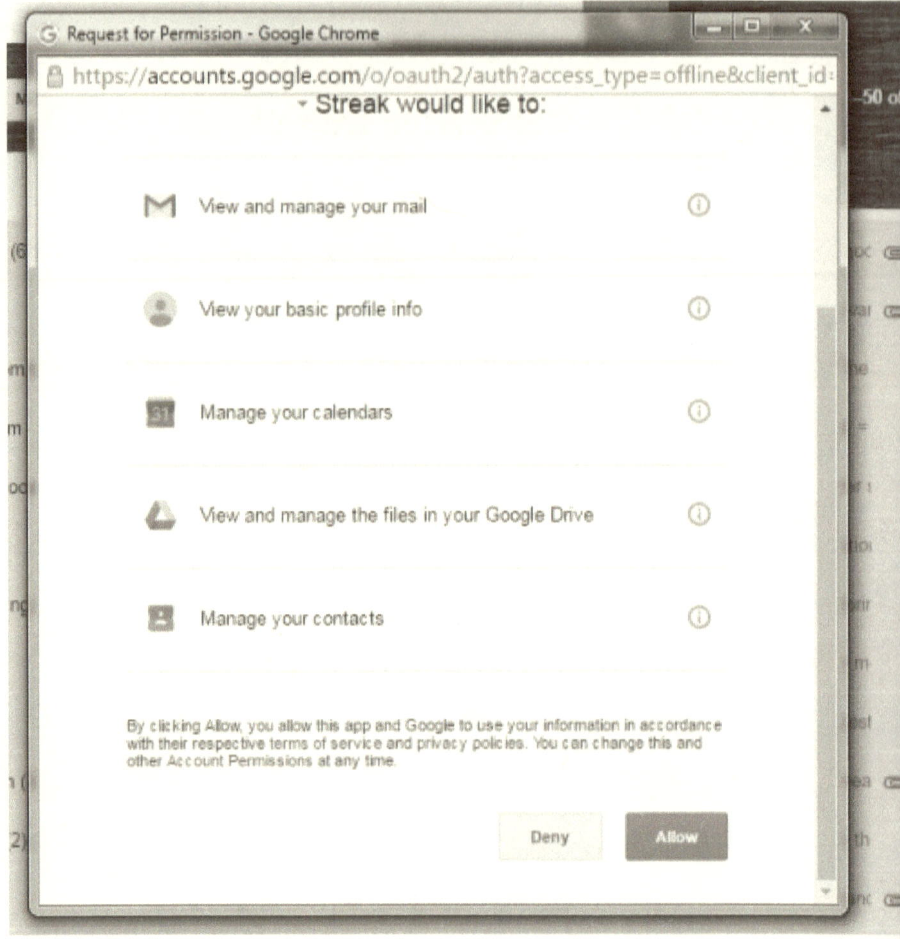

Scroll down and click allow

Then after a few seconds, you can see this in your Gmail's screen (only when logged in through chrome) - like shown in the screenshot

Now reply or compose email to someone. You will see new icons near your send button

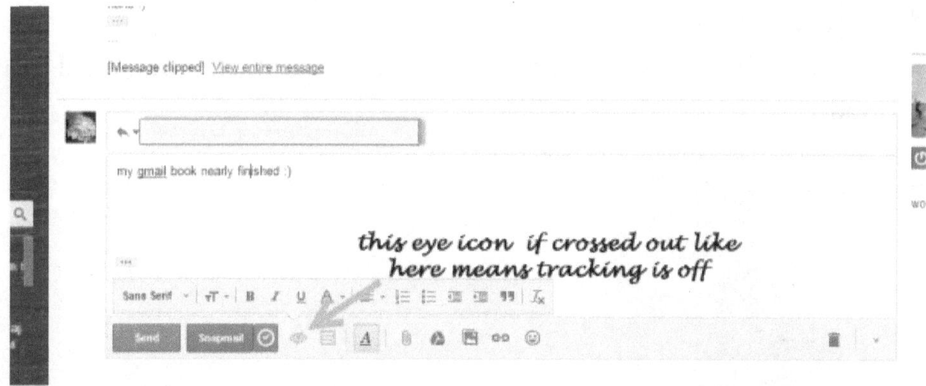

You can to click the eye icon to turn the tracking on; you have to do this for each email separately because you are likely to track only some emails

Note that the eye icon is turned orange it means the email you are sending will be tracked.

Now click send button as usual

If your email is viewed, you will get as notification, from streak

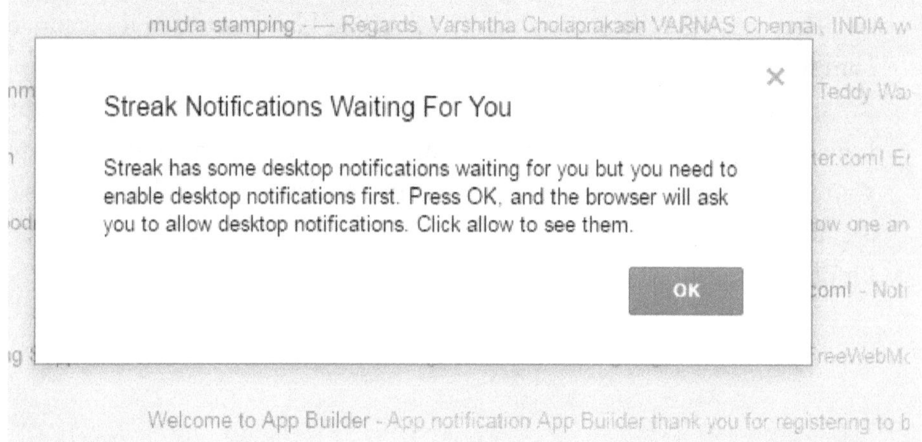

Click okay

You will get desktop notifications from chrome when your tracked email is read

If you miss the desktop notifications, you don't have to worry

You can see links under the sent mail link (as shown below)

Click all tracked email to see the details of all your tracked email

Now you can find whether the recipient has opened your email or not with ease.

There are other services which streak gives; I have not used it personally so I am not covering it here.

In the past four chapters we have been discussing about various functionalities that you can add to Gmail. You can use it in combination to use your Gmail personal account as a fully functional auto responder. (But yes there are limitations to free services – which you may upgrade if you really need to lift of the limits)

Sending Self destructible emails

Sometimes you may need to send some emails which are very secretive in nature and it should get destroyed as soon as possible so that the secret doesn't leak out. You can do this by sending self destructible emails through Gmail

For achieving that function we are going to use a chrome extension which works very well.

You can only send self destructive emails from Gmail using a chrome browser if you don't have Google chrome browser, please download the latest version.

Then go the following webpage in your chrome browser

https://chrome.Google.com/webstore/detail/snapmail/kjoclikoefepdgaplgjlafinekbephji?ref=landing[1]

Click add to chrome

Then you will have to login to Gmail. (From chrome)

Click compose

You will find a new button

---

1. https://chrome.google.com/webstore/detail/snapmail/kjoclikoefepdgaplgjlafinekbephji?ref=landing

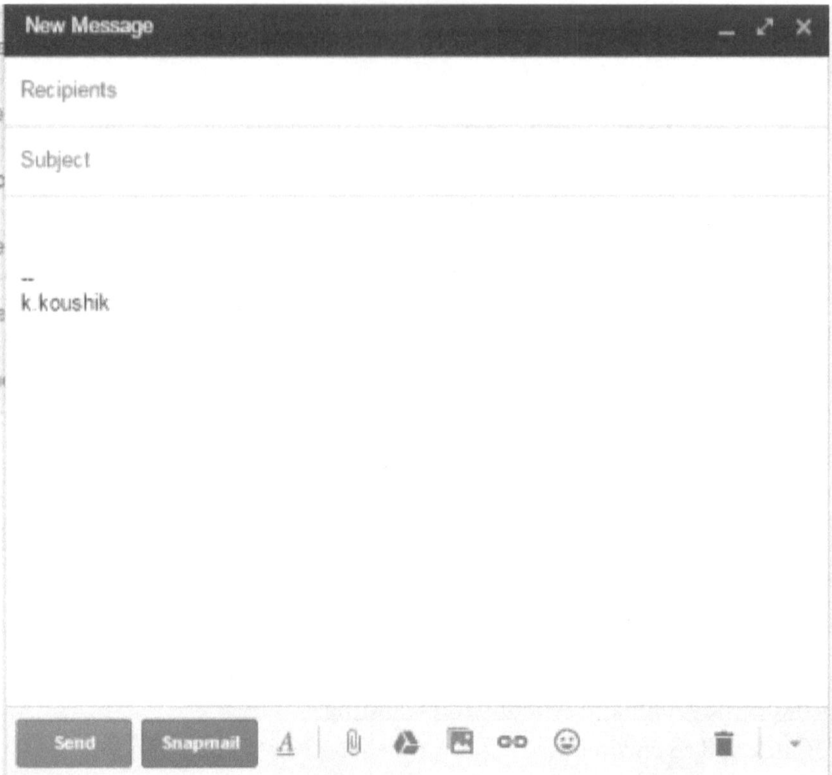

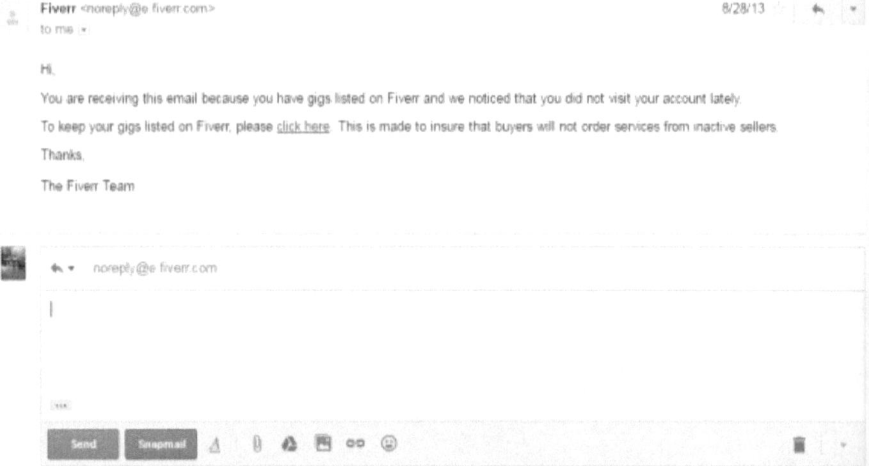

You can also see the same button near send button in replies and forwards also

Now all you have to do is to type your secret message and click snapmail button instead of the send button.

Then your email will go through a secret link and then the message will be self destruct in 60 seconds.

Desktop notifications for multiple Gmail accounts

We have already discussed about desktop notifications before, in this chapter let me show you a cool plug-in for chrome, which achieves the functionality of desktop notifications for multiple Gmail accounts.

https://chrome.Google.com/webstore/detail/checker-plus-for-Gmail/oeopbcgkkoapgobdbedcemjljbihmemj/reviews[1]

Copy and paste the above link in your chrome browser (if you don't use chrome as default)

Click add to chrome

After installing the plug-in you will find the red mail box icon in your chrome browser

Click it and you can access your Gmail any time while working with other web pages

---

1.   https://chrome.google.com/webstore/detail/checker-plus-for-gmail/oeopbcgkkoapgobdbedcemjljbihmemj/reviews

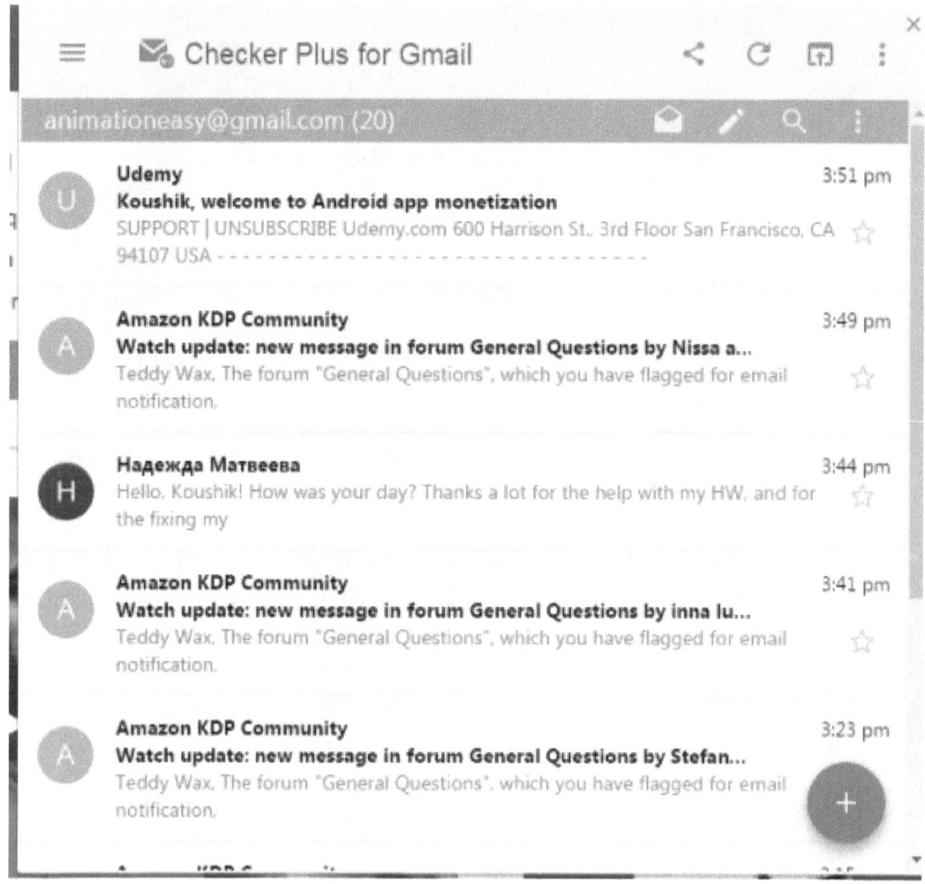

Hover over the email to edit, delete or archive, mark as read unread spam etc

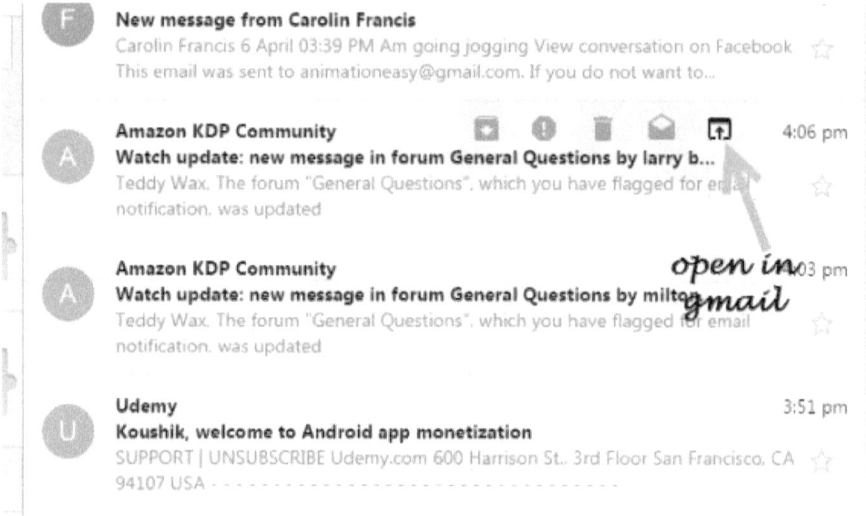

You will get desktop notifications whenever you receive email, you can mark as read or delete from the notification dialog too which makes your work far easier.

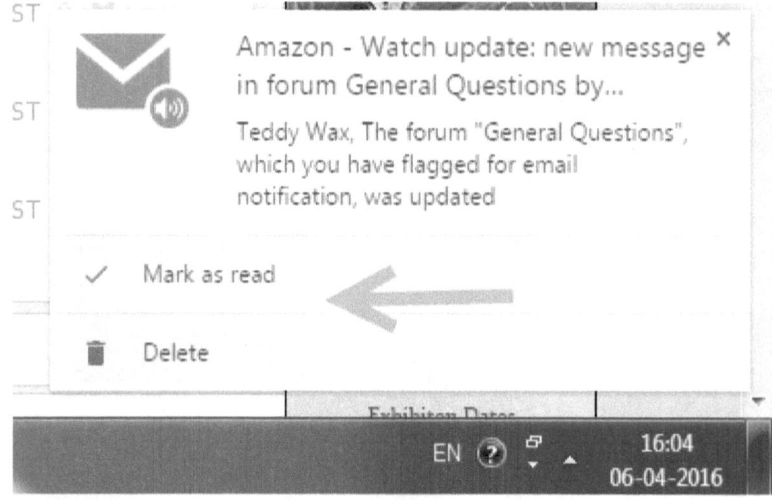

Now to set up multiple email accounts
Click the dotted line
Then click options

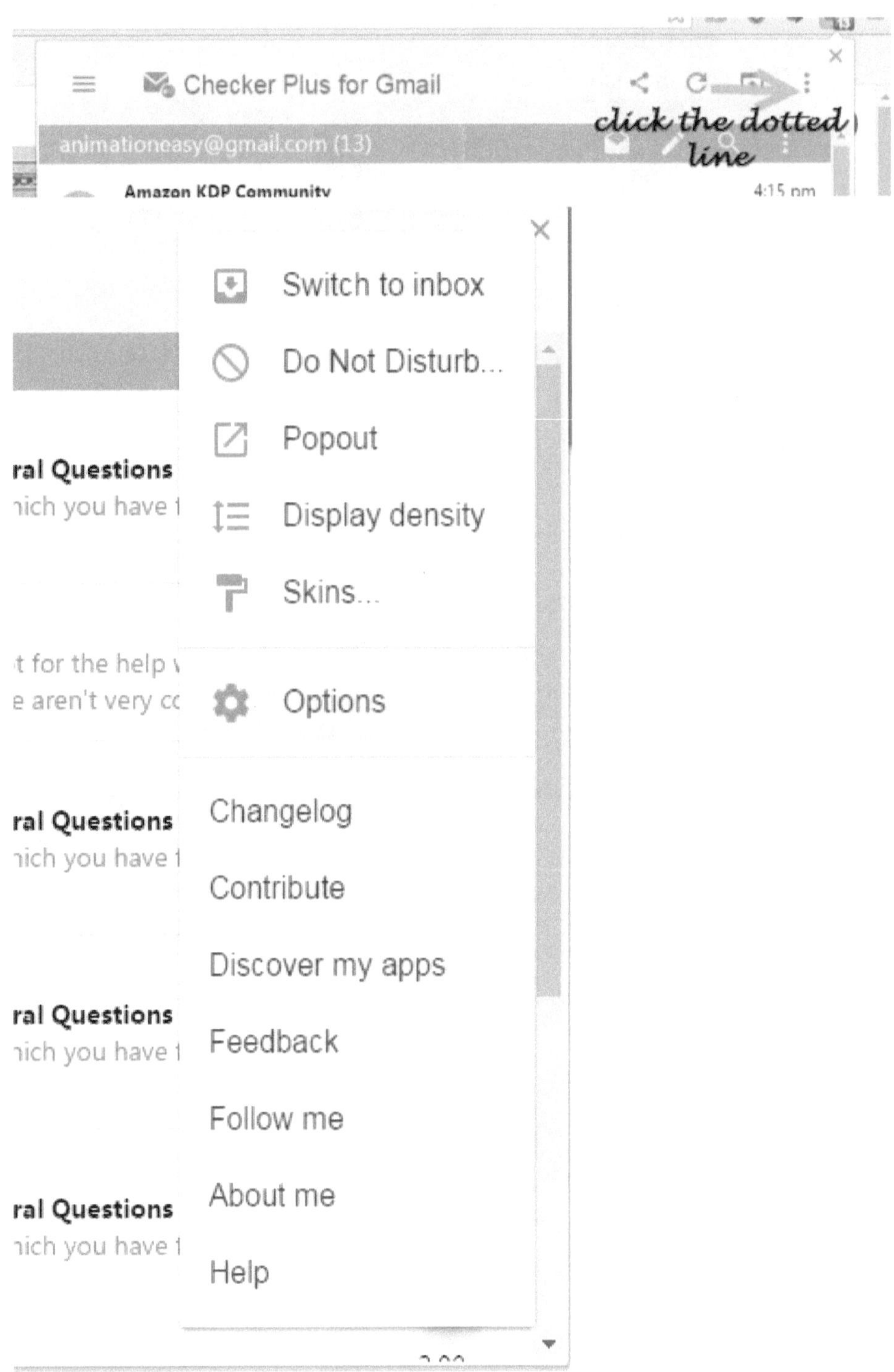
Checker Plus for Gmail
animationeasy@gmail.com (13)
Amazon KDP Community
4:15 pm
click the dotted line
Switch to inbox
Do Not Disturb...
Popout
Display density
Skins...
Options
Changelog
Contribute
Discover my apps
Feedback
Follow me
About me
Help

A mew tab will open

Click accounts/labels

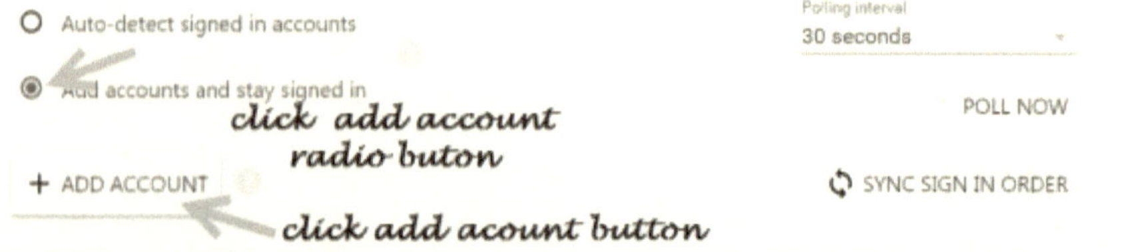

click add accounts and stay signed in radio button

Then click add account button

Gmail login window pops up click add account and sign in to your accounts one by one

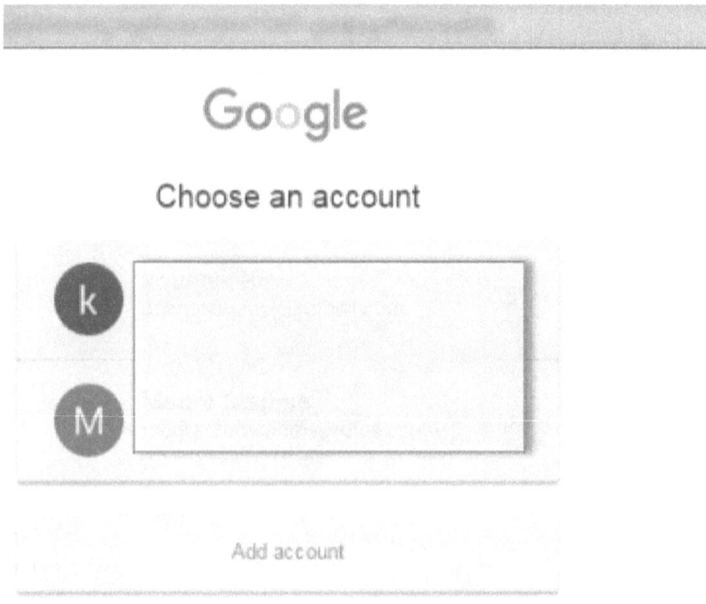

Press the add account link and then login to any Gmail account you want to enable desktop notifications for

Then click allow

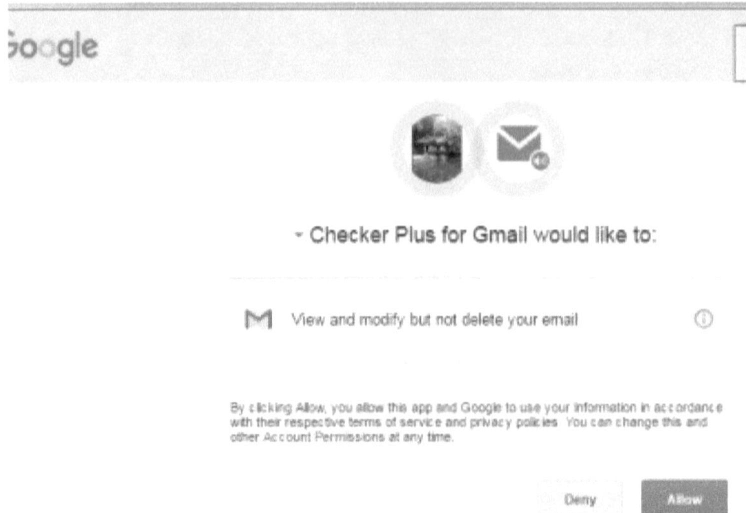

And you are done with setting up desktop notifications for multiple accounts,

Caution: Just remember that the chrome should be running for these notifications to work

Alias emails for Gmail

Though Gmail doesn't offer traditional alias email addresses there is a simple trick which Gmail recommends us to do to get alias emails.

The primary use of alias emails is so that our original email address is still not revealed to the person we are conversing with, or giving our emails to. This is just a small step further in keeping our emails secure from spammers as they still don't know our actual email address. But really Gmail aliases are not that helpful.

In Gmail, you can easily build an alias email using the + operator.

Let's say your email is jack@Gmail.com

You can build thousands of alias addresses just by adding a + sign to end of your username and adding a word.

Jack+email@Gmail.com will still deliver to jack@Gmail.com

Then you have to add that email to your list of emails owned using the accounts and import tab of your settings page – see accounts and import tab chapter for more details

There are really two main problems using this way to create aliases

1. If you give this alias email to a real person he would easily find out that the words before the + sign are your real username.
2. Email forms and other auto-responders can be programmed easily to skip the plus sign and everything after it if the email address submitted is from Gmail.com

Till then you can use this aliases to submit in the opt-in forms to receive gifts (free downloads etc) and then set a filter to delete all other future emails received through that alias email. I know that would be mean. But maybe you would love to do it. ☺

In my opinion the better option would be creating some emails from Gmail.com using the sign up form and then using them as secondary emails. To your primary email account. Then setting up filters as usual. Caution: you may get banned from Gmail if you create a lot of accounts so do it less with caution. You have been warned.

Conclusion

Thank you for completing the book. By Now you know to use Gmail to the fullest. Now it is your part to use your creativity to use the various functions learned in various combinations to suit your needs.

I advise you to check the settings page and change the options according to your need to improve your working speed and productivity.

Feel free to try the new features and email me if you need some help.

Contact Me:

You can always feel free to contact me or send me suggestions, doubts to **writetokoushik@yahoo.com**

138

Please Leave a Review

Thank you for reading the book. Hope you enjoyed it.

If you like this book and enjoyed reading, it would be really helpful if you can share your experience by **leaving a review**[1]

If you have had any problems with the book, please feel free to message me through email **writetokoushik@yahoo.com**

I will try my best to help you with it.

Thank you

K.koushik

---

1. https://www.amazon.com/review/create-review?ie=UTF8&asin=B01B3AT4L6&channel=detail-glance&nodeID=133140011&ref_=cm_cr_dp_no_rvw_e&store=digital-text

Get your Bonus

Please give me your email using the link below and get your bonus eBook

Simple guide to Inbox by Gmail

http://tinyurl.com/gmailinboxguide

I will also update this book when I find some more interesting features, and third party plug-ins to use with Gmail.

Other Books by Author

Kali Santarana Upanishad: An Upanishad from Black Yajurveda which teaches the secret of the holy name of Rama and Krishna

Durga Saptashloki: The Seven Verses from Devi Mahathmyam

Durga Chandrakala Stuti: A Hymn on Durga by Appayya Deekshita: Text with Commentary

Rudrashtakam: A Hymn from Ramacharitamanas by Goswami Tulasidas

Kalabhairavashtakam: Eight Verses on Kalabhairava By Shankara Bhagavadpaada

Sarasvati Ashtottara Shatanama Stotra: Hundred and Eight Names of Sarasvati

Pragyavivardana Stotra - A Hymn from Rudrayamalam: Wisdom Giving Names of Kartikeya Translation Transliteration and Commentary

Shiva Panchakshara Nakshatra Mala: A Hymn on Shiva withStanzas by Adi Shankara Bhagavadpaada

Shadpadee Stotra: A Hymn on Vishnu by Adi Shankaracharya

Ardhanarishvara Stotra: A Hymn on Unified Form of Shiva and Shakti by Shankara Bhagavadpaada

Surya Dvadashanama Stotra

Shiva Panchakshara Stotra

Hundred and Eight Names of Bhairava

Margabandhu Stotra: A Hymn on Margasahaya Shiva By Appayya Deekshita

Ganesha Pancharatnam: A hymn on Ganesha by Shankara Bhagavadpada

Ganesha Sahasranama - Thousand Names of Ganesha: Translated Based on Bhaskara Raya Makhin's Khadyota Bhashya

The Names of Sun God - a Hymn from Mahabharata: Suryashtottara Shatanama Stotra Transliteration, Translation and Commentary

The Heart of Sun God: A Hymn from Valmiki Ramayana: Adithya Hrudaya Stotra - Its Transliteration and Translation

Achyutashtakam: A Hymn on Lord Vishnu by Adi Shankaracharya

Narayana Kavacham: From Srimad Bhagavata Purana

Tales of Hanuman: Tales from the Eternal Life of Hanuman:

Tales of Hanuman: Tales from the Eternal Life of Hanuman:

Hanuman Chalisa Explained

Shiva Manasa Pooja: Mental Worship Of Shiva

Shiva Shadakshara Stotra: A Hymn on Shiva's Six Syllable Mantra

Rama Raksha Stotra: A Shield Of Rama's Names

Names of Shiva: Commentary onNames of Shiva From Shiva Rahasya Khanda Based on Shiva Tatva Rahasya Of Neelakanta Deekshita

Parts of the Body Sanskrit - English: Bilingual Early Learning & Easy Teaching Picture Dictionary: Very useful to understand the meaning of body parts when reciting kavacha stotras & doing anga pooja

Shiva Namavali Ashtakam : An Octet of Shiva's Names by Shankara Bhagavadpaada

The Name of Durga: Durga Nama Anushthana

Heramba Upanishad

Hanumad Bhujanga Stotra: A Hymn on Hanuman in Bhujanga Metre

Durga Saptashloki: The Seven Verses from Devi Mahathmyam(tamil)

Surya Dvadashanama Stotra (tamil)

Durga nama japa vidhi (tamil)

Who Should Start a Membership Business: The Stuff You Need to Know to Run a Winning Membership Business

All That You Need to Know About Tumblr Blogs

All That You Need to Know When Buying Domains

Canva Tips and Tricks Beyond The Limits

Productivity Hacks for Entrepreneurs

Parts of the Body Sanskrit – Hindi - English: Triilingual Early Learning & Easy Teaching Picture Dictionary: Very useful to understand the meaning of body parts when reciting kavacha stotras & doing anga pooja

Partes Del Cuerpo Sánscrito - español: Diccionario de imágenes bilingüe de aprendizaje temprano y enseñanza fácil: Muy útil para comprender el significado ... cuerpo al recitar kavacha (parts of body sanskrit - spanish)

Rama Nama Note with Rama Nama Lekhana Vidhi: Rama-Nama Journal for Writing the Rama's Name , Times Plain Design

Nrusimha Dvadashanama Stotram : Twelve Names of Narasimha

Lakshmi Ashtottara Shatanama Stotra - Hundred and Eight Names of Lakshmi: A Commentary Based on Lakshmi Tantra and Sri Sukta

19 PLUS TIPS FOR USING GMAIL TO THE FULLEST: GMAIL AUTOMATION AND USING THIRD PARTY TOOLS

Les Parties du corps Sanskrit - Français: Dictionnaire bilingue illustré pour un apprentissage précoce et un enseignement facile (parts of body sanskrit French Edition)

Did you love *19 PLUS TIPS FOR USING GMAIL TO THE FULLEST: GMAIL AUTOMATION AND USING THIRD PARTY TOOLS*? Then you should read *Canva Tips and Tricks Beyond The Limits*[2] by Koushik K!

Even for professional designers with training and experience in sophisticated graphic design software packages like corel draw and photoshop, Canva is a quick and easier solution for quality designs with all the ready-made templates, ease of use.For hobby designers or newbies Canva is like a great gift because of its user-friendly, self-explanatory and easy interface.

I once taught Canva a friend who was never inclined towards graphic design and now, he uses it full time to produce graphics for work and personal purposes.

By that experience, I can say Canva is one of the best web applications out there for producing sophisticated designs easily either for social media or for print. Canva's core advantage is its very little learning curve.

---

2. https://books2read.com/u/mdnqaw

3. https://books2read.com/u/mdnqaw

This book will mainly deal with the limitations of Canva and how to deal with them (Legally) without having to pay for it.

Who is this book written for?

Anyone who wants to design quickly and efficiently without much hassle using CanvaAnyone who loves Canva and want to know more about using it efficientlyAnyone who do not wish to buy Canva pro at this time and want to overcome the limitations of Canva (legally)**What will you learn in this book?**

Hidden features of Canva and how to use themCanva tips and tricksCanva secretsWorkarounds for Canva pro only features.Do things you can do only with Canva pro without Canva pro legallyFinding stuff inside CanvaCanva ShortcutsHow to make GIF animations with CanvaUseful resources and their efficient use.

And more...

www.ingramcontent.com/pod-product-compliance
Lightning Source LLC
Chambersburg PA
CBHW021215160726
47994CB00001B/492